Choices and Constraints: Economic Decisionmaking

Choices and Constraints: Economic Decisionmaking

YUNG-PING CHEN, Ph.D.

*Frank M. Engle Distinguished Chair
in Economic Security Research
The American College*

ROBERT C. A. DE VOS, Ph.D.

*Assistant Professor of Economics
Ursinus College*

First Edition ● 1988

AMERICAN INSTITUTE FOR
PROPERTY AND LIABILITY UNDERWRITERS
720 Providence Road, Malvern, Pennsylvania 19355-0770

Foreword

Over the years, the American Institute for Property and Liability Underwriters and the Insurance Institute of America have responded to the educational needs of the property and liability insurance industry by developing courses and administering national examinations specifically for insurance personnel. These companion nonprofit educational organizations receive the support of the insurance industry in fulfilling this need.

The American Institute maintains and administers the program leading to the Chartered Property Casualty Underwriter (CPCU)® professional designation.

The Insurance Institute of America offers a wide range of associate designations and certificate programs in the following technical and managerial disciplines:

Accredited Adviser in Insurance (AAI)®
Associate in Claims (AIC)
Associate in Underwriting (AU)
Associate in Risk Management (ARM)
Associate in Loss Control Management (ALCM)®
Associate in Premium Auditing (APA)®
Associate in Management (AIM)
Associate in Research and Planning (ARP)®
Associate in Insurance Accounting and Finance (AIAF)
Associate in Automation Management (AAM)
Associate in Marine Insurance Management (AMIM)
Certificate in General Insurance
Certificate in Supervisory Management
Certificate in Introduction to Claims
Certificate in Introduction to Property and Liability Insurance

The first CPCU designations were conferred in 1943 to a class of six. Since then, over 22,000 have received this designation by passing ten national essay examinations, meeting an experience requirement, and agreeing to be bound by a Code of Professional Ethics. The American Institute publishes the textbooks and course guides for the CPCU national examinations. This is one of the texts in that series.

As with all Institute publications, this text has been extensively reviewed by a group of academic and industry experts, and they are recognized in the authors' preface. Throughout the development of this series of texts, it has been—and will continue to be—necessary to draw on the knowledge and skills of Institute personnel. These individuals will receive no royalties on texts sold; their writing responsibilities are seen as an integral part of their professional duties. We have proceeded in this way to avoid any possibility of conflict of interests.

We invite and welcome any and all criticisms of our publications. It is only with such comments that we can hope to provide high quality study materials. Comments should be directed to the Curriculum Department of the Institutes.

Norman A. Baglini, Ph.D., CPCU, CLU, AU
President

Preface

This text is designed to introduce CPCU 9 students to some of the major insights of modern microeconomics. Its premise is that there exist natural limitations on the productivity of our economy and on our standard of living. Economic analysis clarifies the choices implied by these limitations. The goal of the book is to develop tools of analysis that not only help citizens evaluate how our economic system deals with these choices, but that can also help them evaluate the choices that confront them as business decisionmakers and as consumers.

Chapter 1 introduces the economic notion of scarcity and provides a model for evaluating its consequences. It explains how scarcity forces us to make choices among alternatives and suggests ways of evaluating the effectiveness of the choices that are made. Chapter 2 investigates how a system of markets can guide the decisions that societies must make with respect to resource allocation. It introduces supply and demand and examines the role that prices play in competitive market economies. Chapter 3 analyzes the way businesses make decisions in market economies. It shows how the profit motive encourages effective use of our limited resources and how these decisions depend on the various types of markets that exist. Chapter 4 formally evaluates the economic implications of competitive markets. It shows how competition can lead to an efficient utilization of our scarce resources. It also identifies some of the limitations of market economies and suggests some remedies for these "market failures." Chapter 5 discusses the logic behind the governmental regulation of markets that fail to work well. Some of the different rationales for regulation as well as limitations on the ability of government to overcome these failures are considered.

Chapter 1 is the joint work of the two authors. Chen is responsible for Chapters 2 and 3, while de Vos is responsible for Chapters 4 and 5.

In addition, each author has read and improved upon the work of the other. That division of labor by two authors who have never met is a tribute to our mutual friend and collaborator, Dr. Robert J. Gibbons, Vice President, American Institute for Property and Liability Underwriters, without whose initial planning, continuing guidance, cooperative editing, admirable patience, and good humor this project would never have been begun, let alone completed.

The authors wish to express their gratitude to the Institute for providing unfaltering assistance in the preparation of the manuscript, which enabled us to work on this book in our spare time while employed full time in other capacities, and to several reviewers for suggesting significant clarifications in the text. In particular, three members of the Economics Department of Villanova University, Alan J. Donziger, Edward J. Mathis, and Charles E. Zech, offered valuable suggestions at a critical time.

These remarks reveal the constraints we faced and the choices we made in developing this book. We leave it to the readers to evaluate the results.

Yung-Ping Chen
Robert C. A. de Vos

Table of Contents

Summary

CHAPTER 1

Economic Decisionmaking

INTRODUCTION

From the financial pages of the press or the business reports on the evening news, it is easy to get the impression that economics involves mostly day-to-day trading activity on the stock exchanges, recent unemployment or inflation statistics, and political debates over the federal budget deficit or tax policy. Although not wrong, this impression is too narrow. Even if we were to add such items as energy, health, farm, or foreign trade policy, we would not begin to see the real significance of economics. No listing of issues or topics alone could ever convey the nature of economics.

Instead of thinking about the particular topics encompassed by economics, it is better to think of economics as an approach—a method of thinking about any number of topics or problems. Economics does not promise a set of solutions to these problems. Rather, it provides a framework within which to analyze them and some tools with which to tackle them. If we learn how to use the tools properly, we can apply them to an endless list of problems.

All the problems or issues we have enumerated somehow concern the quality of life. Most of them arise from attempts to increase (or to keep from deteriorating) the standard of living of particular groups or individuals. For example, U.S. farm policies are designed to increase the standard of living of American farmers. U.S. energy and environmental policies seek to assure Americans today and in the future of dependable sources of energy and an environment that can continue to support human life. A stated objective of the U.S. foreign trade policy is to protect American jobs against "unfair" foreign competition and to

1

open foreign markets to American producers. In short, all of these policies attempt to make some people better off than they would be otherwise.

However, if these policies were only concerned with improving the standard of living, they probably would not generate the intense popular debate they often inspire. After all, who could object to the notion that we should improve the standard of living of our fellow citizens whenever possible? What makes these policy issues such a public concern is the possibility that policies designed to make some particular constituency better off tend to make somebody else worse off. Economic analysis provides the means for comparing the gains and losses that result from such policy decisions.

If we took all the income earned in the United States last year and gave each man, woman, and child an equal share, that amount would come to approximately $15,000, or about $40,000 for an average family of 2.7 individuals. If we assume for the moment that we can redistribute income without reducing the total amount available, then these numbers show that there is enough income generated in the United States to provide a comfortable standard of living for all. But, and this is the key to the problem, there is simply not enough income to make everyone affluent. While most of us could probably survive on an income of $15,000 per person, everyone could surely still draw up a long list of things to buy if only there were more money. At the root of all the problems and issues we have listed lies the simple fact that the output of the American (or any other) economy is limited. This limited output is the reason that the economy's ability to generate income is also limited.

Economists refer to this underlying problem—the problem of limited output and limited ability to generate income—as the problem of *scarcity*. All the issues, problems, and policies considered as economic in origin arise out of scarcity. Precisely because the productive resources and technical capacity of our economy are limited, the exact use of the available resources and technology is a great social concern.

Unemployment becomes a "problem" not so much because we could not put the unemployed on welfare, but because a productive resource—labor—is wasted. Society has to make do with an even smaller "economic pie" (of total production of goods and services) than necessary. The environment becomes a "problem" not because we do not know how to keep it clean or how to clean it up, but because such a cleanup requires productive capacity—people and machines—that otherwise could have been used to make more televisions, newer office buildings, or better schools and hospitals. Foreign trade becomes a "problem" not because we do not know how to protect American jobs from "cheap, foreign competition," but because such protection means that American consumers will probably have to pay higher prices. The essence of resolving these economic problems is choosing the solutions that will bring the biggest gains and the smallest losses possible.

ECONOMICS AS DECISIONMAKING

Economists start from the fundamental notion that our ability to satisfy human wants is limited. The immediate consequence is that choices must be made. Once we make some particular choice, others are precluded. For example, someone who spends a forty-hour week analyzing the local market for real estate cannot simultaneously work on the construction of bridges. Economics involves making decisions about which option will yield the greatest benefits. An economical household provides food, shelter, and other necessities and comforts at the least possible cost. An economical business produces the maximum output from the available resources. Economics analyzes the possible choices, given the constraints of a situation, and enables one to make better decisions as a result.

The analysis of economic phenomena falls into two categories. The first is microeconomics and the other is macroeconomics. *Microeconomics* is the study of economic decisionmaking by individuals, households, or firms, utilizing such concepts as supply, demand, production, and markets. For example, how an individual decides whether to work for a certain wage and how a consumer allocates budget dollars among different purchases are microeconomic questions. How a firm or company decides on production and pricing is another example of microeconomics. *Macroeconomics* is the study of the overall performance of the economy, involving such matters as total output, income, consumption, investment, savings, unemployment, inflation, and recession. These matters relate to the operation of the economy as a whole.

Although this book concentrates on microeconomic issues, there is a close interaction between microeconomics and macroeconomics. In a sense, the separation of the two is artificial, since all economic questions have both dimensions. For example, whether a person decides to work for a certain wage is a microeconomic issue. However, if a larger number of persons than before decides to enter the labor market, unemployment will rise if the demand for labor remains more or less the same. The rise in unemployment is a macroeconomic problem. For another example, how a consumer allocates budget dollars among different purchases is a microeconomic issue. However, if all consumers decide to save less and use more of their income to purchase more goods and services, prices of these commodities will rise if the supply of them is relatively fixed. The increase in the prices of these commodities will be inflation, which is a macroeconomic issue.

The Economic Approach

The economic approach has three distinct elements.[1] First, there is a postulate of *optimization*. Economists interpret human behavior as the outcome of an optimizing strategy; that is, people naturally attempt to achieve the greatest satisfaction of preferences with a given expenditure of resources or to achieve a given level of satisfaction of preferences with the least expenditure of resources. This assumption about human behavior gives economics much of its analytical power.

A second distinct element in the economic approach is the concept of the *implicit market*. Individuals interact in ways that enable them to achieve mutual benefits. Since their wants and needs differ, they can improve their positions by trading with one another. Even without the features of a conventional market, such as money prices and legal property rights, social exchanges occur that tend to move such implicit markets toward an idealized state where everyone is better off.

The third element in the economic approach is the postulate of *stable preferences*. Human beings have certain goals and preferences that they have a strong tendency to try to satisfy, even if those goals are only hazily defined. Such goals and preferences represent an individual's *utility function*, the set or description of those things that are useful or valuable to that individual. Some people seek fame and fortune; others seek happiness and security. Utility is simply a general name for whatever an individual finds satisfying.

These three assumptions provide the basis for the principle of economy that applies in all problem-solving situations from biology to politics. Economizing means using given resources to move as close as possible toward a set of goals or to realize a given aim using as little as possible of the resources required.

All rational choices involve weighing benefits and costs. Such comparisons rest upon the *opportunity cost* principle. Strictly speaking, what is compared is not benefits and costs, but rather benefits and forgone benefits because the opportunity cost of employing scarce resources in one manner is the value of the forgone net benefits of the next best alternative use of those resources. In economics the criterion of efficiency of allocation of resources is fulfilled if the marginal benefit of the project chosen equals marginal cost (that is, the marginal benefit of the forgone "next best" alternative use of resources). Economists compare the costs (forgone benefits) of competing options by converting them to monetary values and discounting the net benefits in each time period to their present value.

Economic theory has been sufficiently powerful, relative to other theoretical constructs in the social sciences, to encourage its extension to many fields outside its traditional domain—political science, sociology, jurisprudence, history, philosophy, and biology. For example, biology and economics deal with similar problems and use comparable principles. Resources, scarcity, and competition together with the laws of nature that govern them apply to all organisms everywhere.[2] Ecology and economics are words derived from the same root. Economic laws apply as much to the natural world as to the world of human commerce. In recent years also, public choice theory has systematically applied the economic approach to matters previously left to political science. This perspective finds rational, selfish, utility-maximizing individuals participating in the political sector just as in the private sector.[3] Public choice theory, or the economic theory of politics, may be summarized as the belief that humans should be considered as rational utility-maximizers in all capacities. It is an economic theory because its "building blocks are living, choosing, economizing persons."[4] Such extensions of economic analysis from abstract models of the business world to wider fields of human endeavor in a sense represent a return to the broad social interests of early economists.[5] While the study of economics has since become more theoretical and mathematical, the economic approach remains a useful method of analysis in many situations. Rational, self-interested choice plays a role in many domains of life other than markets. Some even argue that "it is ultimately impossible to carve off a distinct territory for economics, bordering upon but separated from other social science disciplines. Economics interpenetrates them all and is reciprocally penetrated by them....What gives economics its imperialistic invasive power is that its analytical categories—scarcity, cost, preferences, opportunities...are truly universal in application."[6]

Limitations of the Economic Approach

Formal economic theory, based on rational choice theory, however, applies best to actions in which the consequences affect only the actors who are parties to the action. An individual choice, such as a consumption decision, involves a single actor. In a normal exchange there are two parties, and the exchange has consequences only for those two.

When there are consequences of action for actors who have no control over it, economic theory bogs down. The action in such a case has consequences that cannot be arbitrarily restricted. The central problem that arises in such situations is that these consequences may not be taken into account by the actor or actors making the decision.

The action that yields the best result for the actor may be far from the best for the others who experience consequences of the action. Chapter 4 addresses these problems in greater detail.

Another limitation of the economic approach arises from its assumption of rationality in human behavior. Few people behave rationally all the time, and some people scarcely any of the time. Rationality may fail to govern behavior in two distinct ways.[7] Individuals often commit logical errors even when trying their best to reason correctly. At other times, actions are often "unthinking" because they are governed by habit or passion. To reason strictly in accordance with formal logic can be difficult and complex. On occasion there may be logical lapses that are straight violations of the laws of inference. People also make errors in probability judgments. The human mind often employs rules of thumb that work well most of the time, but which can lead to certain systematic classes of errors. People can also disregard information that does not conform to their existing view. In some contexts people do not even attempt to think rationally or do so only in a very limited way. Habit can be a more efficient guide to action. In many situations habit may be faster and more accurate than thinking. No one can play the piano or drive a car effectively without performing many complex unthinking actions.

The concept of *bounded rationality* introduced by Herbert A. Simon suggests that a person faced with a complex mental task will not attempt to maximize but merely to "satisfice." That is, a person tries to find not necessarily the best solution, but a good one that achieves a given level of satisfaction. According to Simon:

> . . .(a) When performance falls short of the level of aspiration, search behavior. . .is induced. (b) At the same time, the level of aspiration begins to adjust itself downward until goals reach levels that are practically attainable. (c) If the two mechanisms just listed operate too slowly to adapt aspiration to performance, emotional behavior— apathy or aggression, for example, will replace rational adaptive behavior.[8]

Despite these limitations, the study of economics should help to identify the constraints of a situation and the options from which choices can be made. Being able to weigh the costs and benefits of various options effectively makes one a better decisionmaker. Whether the particular decision happens to be some political, business, or even purely personal matter is irrelevant. The study of economics trains the mind to identify options and to evaluate consequences. While they may not always reach the same conclusions, most economists approach problems with the same set of tools and a common way of thinking.

Moreover, in situations requiring economic decisions, logical analysis of the choices available and the constraints imposed may be necessary for survival. If some people make the most of the possibilities open to them, others will fall behind. Clear thinking about such situations is not only desirable for its own sake; it can also be a competitive necessity.

CHOICES

Most of us probably learned at an early age that "everything" was simply not an appropriate response to the question, what do you want? While we may not have realized it at the time, our parents' resources were limited, and they could not provide us with everything we wanted. If asked, for example, "What do you want for your birthday?" we selected something we wanted most. Throughout life we have had to make choices.

At the most obvious level, we are constantly choosing how to spend our money. Do we have enough to take that long overdue vacation? Can we really afford that new car? Or should we be less extravagant and settle for a used model? After all, the money we save now might become a nice nest egg for our retirement. While we can easily appreciate the need to be selective when it comes to spending our money, the need to choose is far more pervasive. That vacation, for example, takes more than money; it also takes time. Someone who uses vacation time to go to Europe for two weeks cannot spend that vacation time on pleasure reading or painting the house.

As these examples show, both as individuals and as society, we always have a menu of choices from which we must select the activities we will pursue. While the menu always has some choices, the set of available options is limited. In other words, there are some things we might wish to do that we are not able to do. Our choices are restricted. The source of the restriction is the scarcity of resources. Scarcity limits our productive capacity and our transformation of nature into what we would prefer it to be. Given such constraints, we try to accomplish as much as possible by making effective choices.

Choice Sets

Economics is largely a study of rational decisionmaking. It provides analytical tools for assessing the relative merits of the available options. It gives us a means of evaluating whether a choice was particularly good or bad or whether it could have been improved upon. This is important not only for the evaluation of individual choices—whether by consumers or by producers—but also for the choices made collectively by society. Economics, by providing ways to define and evaluate the options available, has become an important tool in the development and assessment of social and economic policy.

If we are going to evaluate an action, we must first define the objective of the action. In economics we usually assume that the objective of decisionmakers is to make themselves as well off as possible. It is not rational to choose to make oneself worse off. Of course, we have to be careful when we use phrases such as "well off." What might make one person feel well off, for example, might not appeal to another, and vice versa. People differ in their tastes. Economists usually do not try to assess the rationality of tastes or desires. What matters in analyzing behavior is that the choices lead toward the satisfaction of those tastes or desires. The things consumed that make one feel better off are called *goods* (those things that make one worse off are *bads*). The goal is to choose a bundle of goods that best fulfills our tastes and desires. The same goal exists for society.

Scarcity of resources, however, makes complete satisfaction unattainable. The limitations on the desired consumption of goods defines the choice set. Rational behavior requires that we select from the choice set that combination of goods that fulfills our objectives better than any other combination possible. This means making a choice. Making choices is very difficult because it means that one must give up something in order to have something else. Each choice set involves a tradeoff. In other words, there is always a cost involved in making choices.

In order to have more units of one thing, we must give up some amount of something else. This condition creates the phenomenon of *opportunity costs*. For example, a society may have to choose between military goods and civilian goods, perhaps between tanks and passenger cars. Since similar resources such as rubber, steel, glass, and workers are required to produce both the tank and the car, and since these resources are limited, choices must be made between the two commodities. The cost of manufacturing a tank may be expressed as so many thousands of dollars, but from an economic point of view the cost of manufacturing a tank should be measured in terms of the number of passenger cars sacrificed. Forgoing the opportunity of producing cars makes possible the production of tanks, or vice versa. The concept of opportunity costs shows that pursuing any one option means forgoing some other option.

Fundamental Economic Questions

Since choices are the inevitable consequence of scarcity, there are three fundamental decisions that any economy must make. They involve the questions of *what to produce, how to produce,* and *for whom to produce.* In other words, any society must decide what kinds of output of goods and services to produce, how to organize the inputs of human and capital resources in order to produce the output, and who should get how much of what has been produced. These may be called the economic problems of output, input, and distribution.

There are many ways in which individual and social needs can be satisfied. The goods and services we consume, from necessities such as food and shelter to luxuries such as exotic vacations, determine the quality of our lives. However, since our productive capacity is limited, we cannot provide all things to all people. Choices need to be made. Which "needs" are more important? How we answer this question will partly determine the kinds of goods and services that will be produced. Resources used in the production of shelter are not available for the production of entertainment.

Once we have a notion of the kinds of things that our society needs to produce, we need to decide how to make them. Here again there usually are options. We provide people with food and kitchens in which to prepare meals. Or we can concentrate on the kitchens and provide people with prepared meals that only need minor preparation (such as heating and seasoning) at home. Or we can have everyone eat in restaurants and eliminate the need for home kitchens. The way we answer the question of how things are to be produced has significant implications for the quality of our lives.

Once we have decided what to produce and how to produce it, we must find a way to distribute the output. Do we just divide it equally? Do we try to satisfy the disparate needs of individuals? Do we give first choice to those who worked the hardest? How this distribution issue is resolved affects our standard of living. It is a difficult issue that involves a tremendous amount of subjective judgment. A considerable amount of economic debate revolves around this question of distribution.

CONSTRAINTS

Goods and services or commodities in general are produced in order to satisfy human wants. Two fundamental characteristics of human wants are insatiability and changeability. First, human wants are unlimited. People may start with some basic wants such as foods, shelter, and transportation, but eventually they expand their wants from hamburger to steak, from the first house to the second house, from a bicycle to an automobile. A second characteristic of human wants is that they change over time. The changes may result from changing fashions and quality of the product. If human wants were limited, they would be easier to satisfy with the use of available resources. And if human wants did not change over time, they would also be satisfied more easily. But life is not so simple. If it were, we would not have as much need to study economics.

In other words, we can never find the perfect solution to economic problems and be relieved of the need to make choices. We continually face decisions about how to achieve the most that is possible in any situation. Thus we constantly examine not only the options, but also the limitations. Consumers have only a finite income to spend. Businesses have only a certain budget. Society has only so many resources. Our choices are always made within these constraints.

There are essentially two types of constraints that limit economic decisionmaking. Nature imposes one by limiting the resources available for our use. The scarcity of resources inevitably limits the material possibilities in any situation. The second type of constraint arises from our social and political institutions. We cannot improve our welfare by actions that are illegal. Laws and social conventions represent a limitation on the choices available.

Scarcity

Economics concerns the allocation of scarce resources among competing uses. The point of departure in the study of economics is scarcity. At any one time, an economy has only a limited command over the resources required to produce goods and services. Human wants for goods and services seem to be unlimited, while the resources needed for the production of these things are limited. Therefore, economic decisionmaking tries to satisfy unlimited human wants with the available limited resources. How to allocate limited resources among unlimited wants is the central problem of economics. Scarcity is the basic fact of economic life, and it pervades in all societies. We simply do not have all the resources needed to produce all the things we would want to have. This fundamental constraint is as true in a rich country as it is in a poor country; this same constraint exists in countries with different ideologies. Needless to say, the scarcity phenomenon is more acute in a poor than in a rich country.

If society had unlimited resources, we would not need to pick and choose how to use our resources. If resources were not versatile, then a particular resource could only be used for a particular purpose. Life would be simpler because fewer choices would be necessary. The existence of such choices, however, makes life exciting and difficult all at once. It is exciting because there are so many possibilities; it is also difficult because there are so many possibilities.

If it were not for changing human wants, the economy would run into another sort of difficulty. The particular resources needed to produce the goods and services that people want would be exhausted much sooner than if the demand for goods and services changes. By the same token, the versatility of resources allows them to be used in the production of different goods and services. Scarcity, however, always imposes the ultimate constraint. Scarcity does not necessarily mean that there is very little of something available. Something is scarce when we do not have as much of it as we would want. Something is not scarce if we would not care to have any more of it even if it were offered to us absolutely free. Until a few decades ago, natural gas was not scarce, although fewer reserves had been discovered then than there are today. Before the 1950s there were few commercial uses for natural gas; almost nobody wanted it. Scarcity implies a relationship between availability and desirability. If there is little of it, but nobody wants it, it is not scarce in the economic sense. If there is a large amount of it, but people would like to have even more, it is scarce. A simple test to check if something is scarce is to ask whether or not anybody is willing to pay for it. As a general rule, unless someone is willing to pay, it is not scarce.

The notion of scarcity applies to more than just physical things. Time, for example, is frequently scarce. There are only twenty-four hours in a day. Once certain hours are allocated to a task, those hours are no longer available for anything else. Busy people often hire a secretary because it frees up more of their own time. Homeowners buy timesaving devices such as dishwashers and washing machines because they also have other things to do with their scarce time. With the advent of two-wage-earner families, people tend to eat out more frequently, or at least tend to eat microwave food because they have other things to do with their time than to cook.

Economic Systems

Although all economies face the problems of output, input, and distribution, there is no one method of economic organization that represents the best solution. No two countries operate with exactly the same kind of economic system. Any nation's economic system is one of its manmade social institutions that has evolved over the years. Since societies differ in their social, political, legal, and cultural backgrounds, their economic systems vary as well. Although there are endless variations in possible economic systems, the differences can be clarified by comparing the essential features of a market economy, a command economy, and a mixed economy.

A *market economy* allows a free exchange system where no government or group of individuals interferes with the operation of the market. The question of what to produce is determined by what consumers want, and consumers bid up the prices of those commodities of which they want more. Rising prices thus give the producers the signal about what they should produce more of for the market. In other words, the forces of demand and supply determine what is produced and in what amount. Supply and demand considerations also resolve the problem of how to produce. If labor is relatively cheaper than capital, then more labor, within limits of substitution between labor and capital, will be used and vice versa. The price of labor and the price of capital also depend on the supply and demand of each in the marketplace. The price of labor will be higher per unit if there are relatively fewer persons in the labor force or if there is a relatively great demand for the available labor. The same holds true for the price of each unit of capital. The problem of who gets how much of what is produced will be solved by the income distribution that results in the marketplace. That is, those who contribute more to the production process will be rewarded with a larger income with which to claim more of the goods and services produced in the economy. This system of economic organization is based on property rights, private initiative, and self-interest; its driving forces are competition and consumer demand.

The other extreme may be called a *command economy*. A central planning committee may be set up to direct resources to the production of appropriate goods and services and to distribute them among the people. Such a system depends on complex administrative machinery to collect and analyze the information needed for such decisions and to communicate and enforce them.

Although these descriptions of both systems are greatly simplified, they represent the opposite extremes of economic organization, and there are advantages and disadvantages to each. No current economic system precisely fits either description. The prevailing arrangement may be called a *mixed economy*, where features of both the pure market economy and the pure command economy exist.

The economic system of a country reflects its social, legal, political, and cultural institutions. After World War II, experts from western countries, primarily the United States and the United Kingdom, provided assistance to the underdeveloped countries to help them develop economically, but results were often disappointing. Human societies, much like human bodies, have a "rejection mechanism" that wards off foreign material. Just as a host body rejects a perfectly functioning organ transplanted into it, the host country can reject methods of economic organization that are foreign to it, even though these methods are effective in other lands. In a word, an economic system does not operate in a vacuum.

PRODUCTION POSSIBILITIES

When nature fails to provide to our satisfaction, economic activity begins. A useful way of thinking about production is as a way of transforming nature as we find it into nature as we would like it to be. We can, in fact, produce a change in our environment. Man, of course, is not the only productive animal. Many animals build shelter for themselves or their young. But man has carried the process to the extreme.

Production Processes

Production is the transformation of resources into something that better suits our needs or purposes. We can think of the process most simply as taking some inputs and converting them into outputs. The simplest case is to take a naturally available input (nature as we find it) and to exert some effort to turn it into a consumable good (nature as we would like it to be). When we see an apple tree and climb it to get some apples, we have engaged in production. We have converted nature into a consumable.

There are more complex ways in which production might take place. Rather than wait until we find an apple tree, we might plant and cultivate an apple orchard. It requires considerably more effort, but it should increase the probability of finding apples close at hand. We could, in fact, build a greenhouse in which apple trees can grow year-round. That way we can have apples whenever we like.

Exhibit 1-1 diagrams the productive process in its simplest form. Production starts with certain inputs and transforms them into different outputs by using appropriate production methods or technology.

Inputs Economists generally find it useful to classify inputs and outputs into several categories. A standard classification includes land, labor, and capital. Economists define *land* as any input that is not produced by some human process. It is a nonproduced means of production. Land is nature as we find it. Examples of land include things we normally consider unprocessed natural resources such as virgin forests, iron ore deposits, and the Atlantic Ocean. All of these qualify as land because they are not produced by a human process and they are inputs into production processes (lumber, iron, and ocean transportation, respectively).

Given these two requirements, most farmland is not considered land by an economist because it generally does not occur naturally. It

Exhibit 1-1
The Production Process

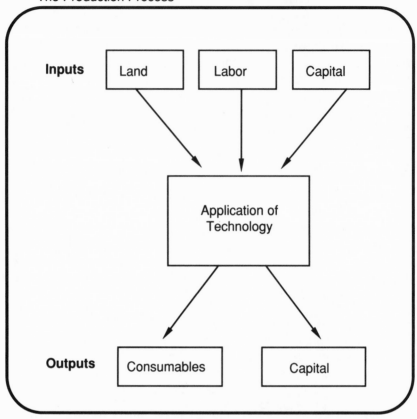

must be cleared, drained, irrigated, and fertilized. In other words, it is itself produced. Icebergs also are not considered land. Although they are not produced by human activity, they fail to meet the second requirement of the definition of land: they are not useful in production. A recent feasibility study assessed the profitability of towing icebergs from the Antarctic to the Middle East as a source of fresh water. If such a project is undertaken, the icebergs will be classified as land.

Capital is a second type of input. It is defined as a produced means of production. An input is capital if it is an output of some other production process. Machinery, factories, tools, and semiprocessed raw materials are all considered capital. The farmland that does not satisfy the definition of land does satisfy the definition of capital. There are also two parts to the definition of capital: the item must have been produced, and it must be an input into some other production process.

Given this definition, money is not considered capital by economists. Money is produced, but it is not an input for production. There really are not any products (other than some jewelry and novelty items) actually made from money. Money is used to facilitate the exchange of goods and services, but it is not a good.

Labor is a third type of input. It is the human capacity to perform work. Animal "labor" is therefore not considered labor. Since domesticated animals do not occur naturally, they are considered capital.

Entrepreneurial talent is also considered a distinct input by some authors. It is the skill of putting together the other factors of production and is clearly indispensable in any flexible, robust economy. However, to minimize the number of categories, we can consider entrepreneurship as labor. This simplification does no damage to the theory of production.

Outputs There are two categories of outputs, consumables and capital. *Consumables* are goods and services produced to be enjoyed for themselves. Food and clothing are consumables. So are medical care and professional football. *Capital* includes goods produced to aid in the production of other goods. As already defined, capital is an output of production that becomes an input into further production. Thus tools, machines, factories, office buildings, and business computers are capital. We may choose to produce capital rather than consumables so that we can produce more of either in the future.

Technology Before we leave the subject of resources we must discuss technology. If we wish to transform inputs into outputs successfully, we must follow an appropriate method. Technology offers a variety of possible methods to achieve the desired result. If we want to create some specific output, we must search through the available technology for an appropriate technique. Which particular technique we use depends on the types and amount of inputs available. As with all things, there is usually more than one way in which any task can be accomplished, and the most suitable technique depends on the relative scarcity of the resources available.

The Production Possibility Frontier

One of the characteristics of modern economies is their success in expanding their consumption possibilities through productive activity. Production is a way of augmenting what nature provides. In simplest terms, it is the manipulation of inputs to generate outputs, where inputs are what is available and outputs are what is desired.

To investigate the properties of a productive economy, it helps to consider a simple model. We assume a simple world in which there are some resources—some land, labor, and capital—and where the technology is such that two kinds of goods can be produced, say beer and pretzels. For simplicity we also assume that there is only one producer, Jane.

If Jane were to dedicate all the resources at her disposal to the production of pretzels, there is some maximum amount of pretzels she can produce. Exhibit 1-2 shows that given the amount of land, labor, and capital available and the particular set of pretzel-producing techniques she has, Jane can produce at most 10 bags of pretzels per day. Of course, she could produce less. Lower production might result from not using all the available resources (unemployment) or from not using the best available technique (inefficiency). Only if Jane operates with full employment and full efficiency can she, in fact, reach the limit of her production possibilities, 10 bags of pretzels per day. But she cannot produce more pretzels unless she acquires more resources or develops a better technique.

Of course, if the technology and the resources are appropriate, Jane should be able to shift some of her resources so that 1 beer can be produced with the resources required to produce 2 bags of pretzels. In other words, if Jane were able to shift just enough resources into beer production to increase beer output from no beer to 1 beer, she would give up 2 bags of pretzels. Resources used for beer production cannot simultaneously be used for pretzel production.

Similarly, if we assume that production of fractional beers and fractional bags of pretzels is possible, the line in Exhibit 1-2 from A to C represents the limit of Jane's production possibilities. The line really is a border or a frontier that separates those production possibilities (combinations of beer and pretzels) Jane can produce from those for which she lacks sufficient resources or technology. All production possibilities inside the frontier are feasible, but she can do better by producing at the frontier.

However, output combinations that lie outside the production possibilities frontier are currently impossible to produce. Jane would only be able to produce them if she had some more resources (land, labor, or capital) with which to work or if she had a better technology with which to put her available resources to use.

The triangle bordered by the production possibilities frontier is Jane's *choice set*. If she is the only person in her economy, then she can consume only the output that she can produce. Even though there are no other people and presumably no need for money, since there is no one to sell to or buy from, it still makes sense to measure the cost of beer or the cost of pretzels. Suppose, for example, that Jane was consuming at Point A (10 pretzels and no beer). If Jane wished to have a bottle of beer, she could not go to the store and buy one. She would have to shift some of her resources out of pretzel production and into

Exhibit 1-2
Jane's Production and Consumption Possibilities

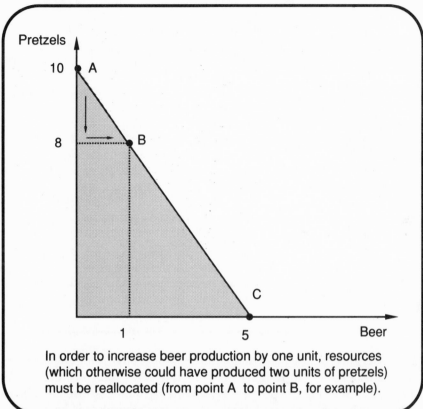

In order to increase beer production by one unit, resources (which otherwise could have produced two units of pretzels) must be reallocated (from point A to point B, for example).

beer production. Since there are fewer resources available for pretzel production, pretzel output must drop. The smallest amount of pretzels that Jane has to give up in order to get her bottle of beer is 2 bags of pretzels. These 2 bags of pretzels represent the true cost of beer to Jane. Her choice, to consume 1 beer, implies another choice, the inability to produce and consume those last 2 bags of pretzels. This is the opportunity cost.

If Jane had chosen to consume no beer, she could have had 10 bags of pretzels. If she chose to produce and consume 1 beer, she could produce at most 8 bags of pretzels. She must give up 2 bags of pretzels if she wishes to consume 1 beer. These 2 bags are the best forgone alternative (use of her resources), and they are the cost of her choice.

We can expand the analysis by considering a second producer-consumer. Suppose that John also has some land, labor, and capital. Suppose that he also knows how to produce beer and pretzels. For the

Exhibit 1-3

John's Production and Consumption Possibilities

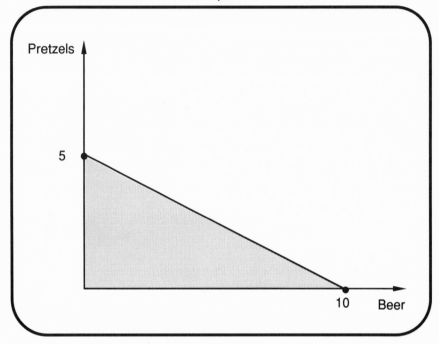

sake of argument, suppose that John's set of production possibilities is the shaded triangle in Exhibit 1-3. Notice that if John were to allocate all his resources to beer production, he could produce at most 10 bottles of beer per day and no pretzels. If, on the other hand, he were to produce only pretzels, he could manage at best 5 bags per day. Although both Jane and John can produce both beer and pretzels, their production possibilities sets are different. Perhaps their skills differ, with John more adept at brewing and Jane at baking, or perhaps their resources are different.

Notice that their costs of production differ. If John were producing only pretzels, he would need to give up only $1/2$ bag of pretzels in order to free enough resources to produce 1 beer. If John were to produce 10 beers, his cost would only be 5 bags of pretzels. If Jane were to give up 5 bags of pretzels, she would only be able to acquire $2\frac{1}{2}$ bottles of beer. It is cheaper for John to produce beer than for Jane, and cheaper for Jane to produce pretzels than for John.

Each additional bag of pretzels costs Jane $1/2$ bottle of beer, while John must give up 2 beers to free enough resources to produce 1 bag of pretzels. These different relative costs of production lead to one of the most powerful arguments for cooperative production rather than self-sufficiency.

Jane's and John's consumption possibilities sets coincide precisely with their production possibilities sets. As long as they operate independently, neither can consume anything other than his or her own output. While both might like to consume 5 bags of pretzels and 5 beers, for example, neither can do so because that production level clearly lies outside their individual production sets.

However, suppose they engage in cooperative production. We can construct a production (and consumption) possibilities set for an economy in which Jane and John cooperate. If they were both to produce only pretzels, world pretzel output could be 15 bags of pretzels per day (Point A). Suppose that they wish to increase beer output. Should Jane give up the production of two bags of pretzels to produce beer? Or should John produce beer at a cost of only $1/2$ bag per bottle?

Clearly Jane should continue specializing in pretzel production while John shifts his talents and resources into beer production. As long as John can expand his beer production more cheaply (that is, sacrificing relatively fewer bags of pretzels), it is efficient for Jane to continue in pretzel production.

This process can continue until John is completely specialized in beer production while Jane continues to produce only pretzels. This puts them at Point B in Exhibit 1-4 where Jane produces 10 bags of pretzels, and John produces 10 bottles of beer. Any further increase in beer production would require Jane's talents and resources. She can, in fact, add an additional 5 bottles of beer to world output at a cost of 10 bags of pretzels. Point C represents a situation where both Jane and John devote all their resources to beer production. No pretzels can be produced.

Notice what has happened. If Jane and John were to pool their production, their collective consumption possibilities set is now the shaded area in Exhibit 1-4. It is possible for both John and Jane to be better off than they were when they were self-sufficient. For example, suppose they decide to produce at Point B. In other words, both John and Jane specialize in the production in which they have a relative advantage. Suppose they divide the output equally. Each could now consume 5 beers and 5 pretzels, a situation that we have already discovered to be infeasible when they operated independently.

As the number of specialized producers increases, the set of production possibilities is likely to have more "flat" segments. The production possibilities frontier might eventually become smoothly rounded as in Exhibit 1-5. This bowed-out shape is called *concave to the origin*. The interpretation of the shape should be straightforward. If we imagine the economy moving from one extreme production possibili-

Exhibit 1-4
Jane's and John's Combined Production and Consumption Possibilities

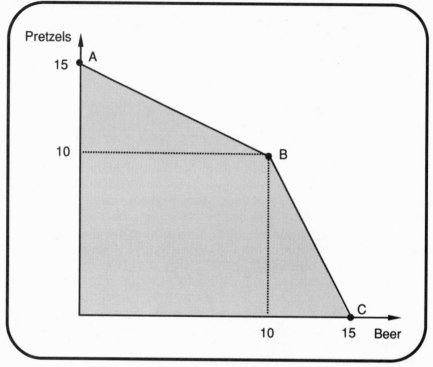

ty, such as Point A in Exhibit 1-5, economic rationality requires that we shift those resources that can increase beer output at the lowest pretzel cost. If we could arrange the resources in terms of the pretzel cost of beer, we would start with the lowest pretzel cost of beer resources and work down to the highest pretzel cost of beer resources.

The concavity of the production possibilities frontier tells us that every unit increase in beer production requires us to forgo increasingly large amount of pretzels. While the first beers might cost us relatively few bags of pretzels, the last beers will cost the most. This phenomenon is known as the *law of increasing relative cost.*

Expansion of Production Possibilities

There are several ways in which choice sets can be expanded. If we have more resources to work with, our productive capacity should increase. The amount of land available in the world is relatively fixed. It certainly cannot be increased through our own productive efforts. It

Exhibit 1-5
The Production Possibilities Curve

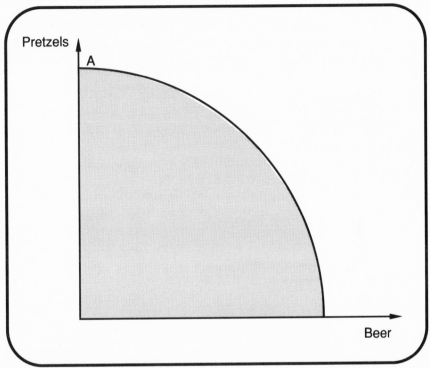

can, however, be increased indirectly. Since natural gas once did not have any economic uses, it was not considered land. If we can find ways of putting to use some previously unused natural resources, we will have expanded our land.

A recent example occurred in the 1970s when efforts turned to finding alternative energy resources. Solar and wind energy have been available since the beginning of time, and they have been tapped for productive purposes at various times. The Dutch harnessed wind power to drain a considerable portion of what is now extremely fertile farmland. The energy crisis of the 1970s stimulated significant attempts at commercial solar and wind energy generation elsewhere. Today, a significant portion of the electricity distributed by Southern California Gas and Electric comes from such nontraditional sources. Shale from the Rocky Mountains, although quite useless today (and therefore not considered land), might become an important fossil fuel source in the future.

A closely related way of expanding our choice sets is to make our available resources more productive through technological improvements. If we could find better ways to combine resources, their productive capacity could be greatly expanded. Technological advances in transportation and communication have greatly increased labor productivity. Imagine the difficulties of coordinating production in different regions of the country in the days of Benjamin Franklin, when as simple a trip as from Boston to Philadelphia usually required more than a week. Now someone can go from Washington, D.C., to London, England, in just over three hours. But modern telecommunications networks make it possible to transact business around the world without leaving the office. Resources can now be used more efficiently as a result of developments in computer technology. Machines that can carry out millions of mathematical operations in a single second have replaced many people with adding machines.

Another way to expand the production possibilities is to invest in more capital. If we sacrifice production of some consumable goods and instead increase our supply of capital, our future productivity can be increased. Panel A in Exhibit 1-6 shows the production possibility when the two types of goods produced are capital goods and consumer goods. The amount of consumer goods that we produce determines our current standard of living. The amount of capital that we produce today determines the size of our choice set in the future.

An economy that continually produces at Point A will have a relatively high current standard of living. But it will add nothing to its capital stock. A society that produces at Point B will forgo some present comforts but will add more capital to its supply of resources. Panel B in Exhibit 1-6 suggests how the growth path of an economy might depend in part on the political structure and social characteristics of the country. The United States, for example, tends to emphasize living well in the short run. Since the savings rate is low, while current consumption is high its production possibilities might expand from Point B to Point B'. In Japan the growth rate is higher. People postpone present consumption, freeing resources for capital formation. Thus Japan's production possibilities might expand from Point C to Point C'. In some societies the political system can force savings on the part of the people (through shortage of consumer goods) and increase the growth rate.

A national growth rate is largely a matter of choice. To increase the growth rate, society must be willing to forgo consumer goods in order to create capital. In other words, society must save more in order to invest more. Depending on our tastes or the preference of economic decisionmakers, the growth rate will be larger or smaller.

Exhibit 1-6
The Expansion of Production Possibilities

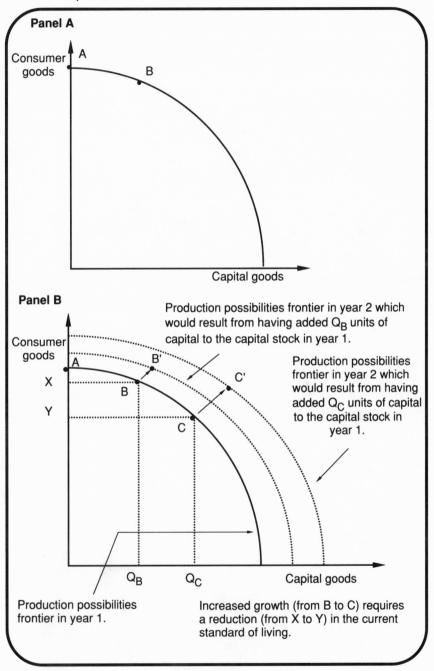

SUMMARY

Economics, by providing a systematic approach for analyzing the choices and constraints of various situations, offers powerful tools for decisionmaking. Its power in analyzing situations and predicting human behavior comes from three fundamental assumptions. Economists assume that people act rationally to maximize their utility, that they interact in an implicit market, and that their goals and preferences are relatively stable. In other words, they know what they want, they make trades with one another to get what they want, and they choose only those trades that get them closer to what they want. Rational maximizing behavior means simply making the most out of the possibilities, or in a word, economizing.

The attempt to make the most of the possibilities recurs in so many situations that the economist's analytical approach has been extended to many other fields, from biology to politics. The complexities of the world make it impossible to measure accurately all the variables in a situation, and even then people do not always act rationally. Reason prevails often enough, however, that the analytical tools of the economic approach can be applied to almost any situation and enable one to make better decisions as a result.

Decisions are choices between alternatives. Choosing one option means sacrificing another option. The options available in any given situation represent the tradeoff or the choice set. A rational decision involves weighing the costs and benefits of each alternative. The cost of an option is the same as the forgone benefit of the next best alternative. Thus all costs are opportunity costs—the potential benefits that must be sacrificed.

For any economy as a whole, the choices can be expressed as three fundamental questions. The first is, *what* should the economy produce? Of all the possible goods and services that could be produced, which ones does the society want the most? The second is, *how* to produce? Of all the technology available, which production methods are the most efficient. The third question is, *for whom* to produce? Of the total output produced, how much should go to each individual?

The need to make such choices stems from the inescapable constraints that always limit the possibilities. Some of these are constraints of nature. Although nature provides resources that can be transformed into the desired goods and services, these resources are scarce. Because they exist only in finite quantities, the potential output is also limited. Other constraints result from the laws and customs that govern society. No two countries have exactly the same economic system. Economic systems range from a pure market economy, in which a completely free market allocates resources, to a command economy, which allocates all resources through a central planning mechanism. Most countries have mixed economies.

These natural and political constraints limit the production possibilities open to any economy at a particular time. Production transforms certain inputs into desired outputs. The production possibilities represent a choice set. The economy can produce more of one type of output or more of another, but not both unless it still has unutilized resources. The tradeoff is that it must sacrifice some of one to gain more of the other. The limit on the various combinations of output that are possible is the production possibilities frontier. Although this frontier is fixed at any specific time, it can be expanded outward over the course of time. The discovery of new resources, the development of more efficient technology, or the investment in more capital will ultimately shift the production possibilities frontier outward and expand the range of choices available to the society.

Good decisions in regard to such choices rest on clearly identifying the tradeoffs. Chapters 2 and 3 analyze the choices facing buyers and sellers in the marketplace and producers in managing a business. Chapters 4 and 5 examine the choices facing society as a whole in relying on the market system to allocate resources or imposing regulation on the operation of the economy.

Chapter Notes

1. Gary S. Becker, *The Economic Approach to Human Behavior* (Chicago: University of Chicago Press, 1976).
2. Jack Hirshleifer, "Economics from a Biological Viewpoint," *The Journal of Law and Economics,* April 1977, pp. 1-52.
3. James M. Buchanan and Gordon Tullock, *The Calculus of Consent* (Ann Arbor, MI: University of Michigan Press, 1962).
4. James M. Buchanan, "The Economic Theory of Politics Reborn," *Challenge,* March/April 1988, p. 4.
5. Buchanan, "The Economic Theory of Politics Reborn," p. 10. Hirshleifer, "Economics from a Biological Viewpoint," p. 3.
6. Jack Hirshleifer, "The Expanding Domain of Economics," *The American Economic Review,* December 1985, p. 53.
7. Hirshleifer, "Expanding Domain," pp. 59-61.
8. Herbert A. Simon, "Theories of Decision-Making in Economics and Behavioral Science," *The American Economic Review,* June 1959, p. 263.

CHAPTER 2

Buying and Selling Decisions

INTRODUCTION

Every society faces fundamental economic decisions in allocating its resources. In 1776 in *The Wealth of Nations*, Adam Smith pinpointed the primary advantage a market system offers for making those decisions.

> Every individual...endeavors...to employ his capital...so that its produce may be of greatest value....He generally...neither intends to promote the public interest, nor knows how much he is promoting it....He intends only his own security,...only his own gain. And he is in this...led by an invisible hand to promote an end which was no part of his intention...By pursuing his own interest he frequently promotes that of society more effectually than when he really intends to promote it.[1]

Although much has changed since Smith presented this concept, most economists believe that it still has great relevance to our modern mixed capitalist economy. Of course, there are important areas where the market fails, and government intervention is required. Even when the market is working competitively and efficiently, there is no guarantee that everyone will regard the resulting distribution of income as fair. Here, too, government may be called on to reduce the degree of inequality generated by the market. In most situations, however, the market mechanism is more likely to respond quickly and sensitively to changing consumer preferences and changing resource endowments than are central planners, even those benevolently motivated.

In a free market, individual decisionmakers observe prices and decide whether to buy or sell accordingly. The price system is a remarkable information system. In a competitive market economy prices transmit information between producers and consumers. Without any central planning, resources are continually reallocated in response of those information signals. Although each producer is motivated by self-interest, the result is to promote consumer welfare. It is little wonder that Adam Smith wrote that such a process must be guided by an invisible hand.

Many important economic decisions are responses to these price signals. Prices indicate the relation of the forces of supply and demand in the marketplace. When market conditions change, prices provide the first clue. Decisionmakers must be able to interpret these clues if they are to respond effectively. A particularly important issue involves the sensitivity of the market to price changes. The *elasticity of demand* measures the effect on the quantity demanded of a change in the price of the product. Whether such a price change will increase or decrease a firm's total revenues is a crucial question for the firm's decisionmakers. Thus these fundamental economic concepts often suggest the appropriate business strategy.

SPECIALIZATION AND EXCHANGE

Chapter 1 illustrated how cooperative production can increase the total output of an economy and thus improve the standard of living for its customers. However, this improvement in the standard of living is impossible without exchange. To exploit the relative advantages different individuals have, trade must be a relatively easy process. Thus a well-functioning, efficient economy requires an effective and reliable monetary system; otherwise trade could be little more than direct barter.

In a barter system each producer must find another producer whose needs and supplies are exactly opposite of his or her own. The beer specialist who wants pretzels must find a pretzel specialist who wants beer. Economists refer to this condition as a *double coincidence of wants*. In an economy that produces only beer and pretzels, this double coincidence might occur frequently. But imagine the problem of bartering in an advanced economy where there are specialists in the production of literally millions of commodities.

One of the reasons for the tremendous productivity of the American economy is the extreme degree of specialization of its workforce and other resources. Most of us work, but not everyone actually produces some well-defined commodity. Many of us perform extremely specialized tasks in a corporate setting that collectively might not even produce a final consumer good. Almost none of us would be able to survive without the output of others. Certainly, very few would be able to exist at anywhere near our current standard of living.

Essential Features of a Market System

Specialization works only because each person's output can be exchanged for another's in a smoothly functioning market. For markets to function, however, certain conditions are essential. Among these are property rights, freedom of enterprise and choice, and diffusion of economic power.

Property Rights Property rights exist when the legal system enforces an individual's exclusive ownership of certain resources. The essence of private property rights is the transferability they impart to claims to the value of certain goods and services. The extent to which the things that have use-value, whether in production or in consumption, are privately owned and easily transferable is one characteristic that distinguishes a capitalist economy from a socialist economy. The types of commodities in which individuals may have property rights is partly a function of custom, law, and technology. As such, they are not immutable and do, in fact, change.

It is common for us to think of land, for example, as a perfectly reasonable type of private property. Yet this has certainly neither always been true, nor is it currently true in many societies. Even in the United States, considerable tracts of land are held by the government, and it is impossible for private individuals to obtain private property rights to them. In fact, the very notion that land could be bought and sold is a fairly recent development in the western legal system. Even today, the right to sell land is severely restricted in a number of western countries.

Ownership of scarce and valuable resources is essential for the efficient functioning of the price system. Prices convey information about the resources used to make each product only because producers must pay the owners of those resources in order to obtain them. This private cost is then passed on to consumers in the price of the product.

To work well, then, the price system requires the enforcement of property rights so that ownership of inputs is recognized and respected, and producers are legally able to use inputs only when the owners of those inputs agree to supply them. Owners, of course, will make supply available only if they receive what they regard as adequate compensation.

Freedom of Enterprise and Choice Markets allocate resources best when the participants are free to buy and sell according to their own decisions about what is best. There are no artificial obstacles to entering or leaving a particular line of work or a particular type of business. Individual rather than institutional decisionmaking prevails, and individuals have the freedom to implement those decisions.

Diffusion of Economic Power Markets depend on competition to establish the best price. Buyers bid against each other, and sellers against each other. For such a system to work, there must be a large enough number of independent participants so that no one of them can control the outcome. Individual buyers and sellers are then able to transact business with whoever offers them the best price.

Circular Flow of Economic Activities

The operation of the economic system may be viewed as a circular flow of activities. There are two kinds of markets involved in this flow, *product markets* and *resource markets*. A market is simply an environment or place where the producers and consumers get together in trade. In the product market goods such as food, clothing, houses, automobiles, and stereos, as well as services such as home and auto repair, medical care, legal assistance, and investment advice are exchanged. These goods and services are outputs of production. Labor and capital are exchanged in the resource market. These resources are sometimes called factors of production or inputs into the production process. In spite of this distinction, however, the product market and the resource market continually interact. They are interdependent because, for example, the availability of a particular commodity depends on the availability of the resources for producing it. In addition, individuals generally earn their income when they offer their resources in the resource market, and they spend that income in the product market to buy commodities. Exhibit 2-1 illustrates the circular flow of activity between the two markets.

The major sectors of the economy are *households, businesses,* and *government.* The *household sector* comprises consumers and owners of resources. Production occurs in the *business sector* where capital and labor are organized into the production process. *Government* also hires labor and produces services, but its motivation differs from that of the business sector.

THE MARKET MECHANISM

People's preferences for products are constantly changing. An efficient economy should respond to these changing preferences by varying the mix of products actually produced. If consumers decide

Exhibit 2-1
Circular Flow of Economic Activity

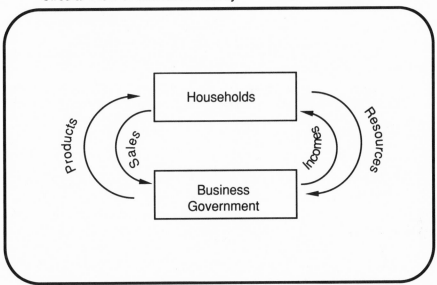

they want more of product A and less of product B, an efficient economy would respond by shifting the factors of production—land, labor, and capital—from industry B to industry A, enabling consumers to obtain the mix they now prefer. Because the market decentralizes decisionmaking, it processes information more efficiently than a central planning system. Each producer observes only the prices of the resources he or she needs and the products he or she sells. With this information the producer tries to maximize profit. The market, through the interaction of supply and demand as registered by price changes, coordinates the activities of thousands of producers without any central planning or direction. This process allocates resources without any group of individuals being required to process information on thousands of products and factors of production.

Producers do not try to satisfy customers to promote the public interest. They only try to promote their own self-interest. Yet the result of the competitive market process, driven by the profit motive, is to allocate resources in exactly the direction that consumers desire. In the end, consumers enjoy more of product A and do with less of product B, just as they wish.

The market mechanism organizes both the production and the distribution of goods throughout the economy. The same mechanism functions in the product market and in the resource market. Business firms and governments are sellers of goods and services, but buyers of inputs. Households sell labor and buy goods and services.

The prices determined in these markets allocate resources among potential users. Market prices serve as a rationing device. Only those buyers who are willing and able to pay the market price (or more) will get the resources they want. Others will have to do without. Similarly, only those sellers who are willing and able to supply commodities at the market price or less will make any sales. Thus the individual decisions of many households, firms, and government agencies guide a free market economy in an efficient and seemingly invisible manner.

Demand and Supply

Markets determine prices through the interaction of demand and supply. The interests of consumers and producers meet in the market. Each participant is free to accept or reject any offer. The outcome of this bargaining process depends on the forces of demand and supply.

Demand Demand is a shorthand expression for *demand schedule* or *demand curve*. It relates the price of the product to the quantity demanded of that product. The demand curve has a negative slope because there is an inverse relationship between the price of the product and the quantity demanded.

Demand depends on tastes and preferences, income and wealth, prices of other commodities, and price expectations. Tastes and preferences indicate the current choices consumers are likely to make if everything else is equal. Income and wealth influence the ability of consumers to buy various commodities; at higher levels of income or wealth, their purchases of luxuries as opposed to necessities are likely to increase. Prices of other commodities influence the choices between one commodity and another. Price expectations influence the decision whether to buy now or to wait for a more favorable price in the future. Variations in these four factors account for the difference in demand by different individuals. If we examine the total market demand for a commodity (such as housing), then the number of consumers (renters) becomes an additional factor to consider.

Exhibit 2-2 illustrates the quantities demanded by various consumers in a hypothetical example. The first column shows five possible prices per unit of this commodity: $5, $4, $3, $2, and $1. Each of the three columns for Consumers A, B, and C shows the number of units of this commodity that each consumer will purchase at the various alternative prices. In fact, reading across shows that at a price of $5, Consumer A will buy one unit of this product, Consumer B will buy two units, and Consumer C will buy three units. At a unit price of $4 apiece,

Exhibit 2-2
Hypothetical Demand Schedule

Price of the Product	Quantity bought by:			
	Consumer A	Consumer B	Consumer C	All Consumers (market demand)
$5	1	2	3	6
4	2	3	4	9
3	3	4	5	12
2	4	5	6	15
1	5	6	7	18

the respective amounts that Consumers A, B, and C will buy are two, three, and four units. What explains the different amounts that these consumers will buy at the same price? According to the four preceding factors, it may be that Consumer C likes this commodity more than Consumer B or A does; or Consumer C has more income or wealth than Consumer B or A does. It may be that the prices of *other* commodities that Consumers A, B, and C normally buy affect their purchases of the commodity in question. Last, perhaps these consumers have different expectations about how the price of this commodity will change. It may be that Consumer C buys more units of this commodity because Consumer C expects the price of this product to rise more than Consumer A or Consumer B expects it to rise.

The last column in this table shows market demand, which is a horizontal summation of the quantities Consumers A, B, and C combined will purchase. In this model we assume that these three consumers constitute the entire market. Adding these quantities together produces the demand curve shown in Exhibit 2-3.

Why is there an inverse relationship between the price of the product and the quantity of it demanded? This inverse relationship expresses the tendency for the value of a commodity to any one person to decrease as the quantity of that commodity obtained increases. The more units of a particular commodity that someone has, the less important an additional unit becomes. If the price paid for a product represents the sacrifice, then it makes sense that a person will be willing to sacrifice less (or pay a lower price) for something of lesser

Exhibit 2-3
Hypothetical Demand Curve

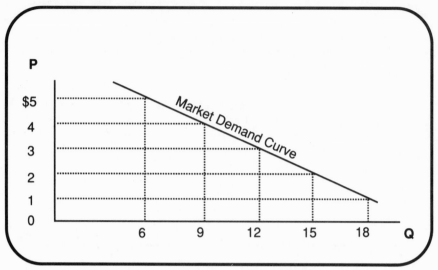

value. In other words, one way to induce a person to buy more units of something is to offer a lower price so that the buyer sacrifices less. This tendency is also known as the *law of diminishing marginal utility*, which explains the downward sloping demand curve.

Supply Supply is a shorthand expression for *supply schedule* or *supply curve*. It expresses the relationship between the price of a resource and the quantity of that resource supplied at those prices. Unlike the demand curve, the supply curve has a positive slope. The slope is positive because there is a *direct* relationship between the price of the commodity and the quantity of that commodity the suppliers offer for sale. Given the cost of production, the higher the price of a product is, the greater will be the spread or difference between cost and revenue, namely, profit. This increased profit is the incentive for suppliers to offer more for sale.

The factors that determine supply include the technique of production, the prices of the resources, the prices of other commodities, and price expectations. When we refer to the total supply in the market, the number of suppliers or producers will be an additional factor to consider.

Exhibit 2-4 shows a hypothetical supply schedule for Producers A, B, and C. Exhibit 2-5 graphically presents the same information. It shows a supply curve relating the price of the product to the quantity

Exhibit 2-4

Hypothetical Supply Schedule

Price of the Product	Quantity Offered by			
	Producer A	Producer B	Producer C	All Producers (Market Supply)
$5	5	6	7	18
4	4	5	6	15
3	3	4	5	12
2	2	3	4	9
1	1	2	3	6

Exhibit 2-5

Hypothetical Supply Curve

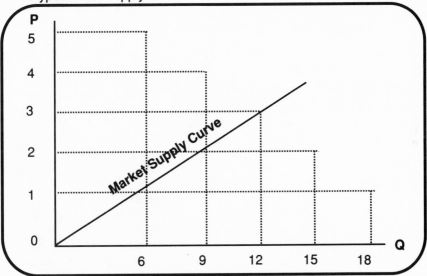

supplied. The upward slope indicates that as the price rises, the quantity offered for sale increases.

Equilibrium, Shortage, and Surplus

Market *equilibrium* occurs when the quantity of a commodity that consumers would like to purchase at a *given* price equals the quantity

Exhibit 2-6
Hypothetical Demand and Supply Schedule

Price of the Product	Quantity Demanded	Quantity Supplied
$5	1	5
4	2	4
3	3	3
2	4	2
1	5	1

the producers would like to sell at that price. This situation *clears the market* so there are no unsatisfied buyers or sellers. A *shortage* occurs when at a given price the consumers would like to buy more than what the producers would like to sell. A *surplus* occurs when at a given price producers offer more for sale than consumers care to purchase.

These three market phenomena are illustrated by the table in Exhibit 2-6. In this hypothetical example the quantity demanded equals the quantity supplied when the price of the product is $3. The supply and demand diagram in Exhibit 2-7 shows the same result: the supply curve and the demand curve intersect at a price of $3 and a quantity of twelve. At any other price there are unsatisfied buyers (a shortage) or unsatisfied sellers (a surplus).

If the market is free to adjust, the price of the product moves toward the equilibrium level when there is neither a surplus nor a shortage at the existing price. If there is a surplus when the price is $5, for example, producers will compete among themselves by lowering the price in order to sell more. Eventually the equilibrium price that clears the market will be reached. At that price both consumers and producers want to trade the same quantity of that commodity. If there is a shortage at the price of $1, for example, consumers will compete with one another to obtain the product by bidding up the price until the equilibrium price is reached.

Equilibrium does not always exist in a free market. Because the fundamental market forces of supply and demand always change, even if equilibrium is reached, it will soon be disturbed. In other words, the development of a shortage or a surplus in the market is natural, but these disequilibrium conditions are normally temporary because the market will adjust to reach a new equilibrium.

However, a shortage or surplus can be chronic. This situation can occur if government tries to fix prices or quantities, interfering with the normal adjustment of the market. For example, the government may

Exhibit 2-7
Hypothetical Market

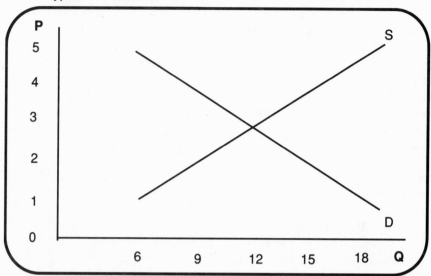

consider the price of housing (apartment rental) in a city or an area in the city as too high for the welfare of the renters and can decide to impose rent control. This act will create a shortage of apartments until the restriction is eliminated. It becomes a chronic condition because price mechanism is not permitted to allocate the scarce commodity. Such *price controls* interfere with the flow of information between producers and consumers and inhibit the reallocation of resources in the direction preferred by consumers.

In unregulated equilibrium, which occurs where supply and demand intersect, consumers can buy as much as they want at the going market price. There is no excess demand or shortage. Thus people with an "urgent" preference may obtain as much as they are able and willing to buy.

In our economy, where most prices are unregulated, we normally take for granted that adequate supplies will be available if we are willing to pay the going price. We are irked when we occasionally learn that the store is out of our chosen item, but this situation is the exception.

Under price control, however, buyers cannot obtain as much as they want at the going price. Who, then, gets the available supply? It would be desirable, of course, if buyers with the most "urgent" preference received the limited supply and those with more frivolous demand were excluded. But this may not be the case. Available supply may be allocated on a first-come, first-served basis. Some buyers with frivolous demand may get as much as they want. Others with a desperate desire for the product may get little or none.

For example, under rent control, some lucky households with only a weak preference for residing in the controlled locality may obtain a low-priced apartment. If rents were decontrolled, even a modest rise in rent might induce such households to move to another locality. However, some unlucky household with a strong desire to reside in the controlled area may be simply unable to find an apartment. Under decontrol, price would rise until the market clears. Those with a weaker preference would be deterred by the higher price; those with a strong preference would be able to obtain an apartment.

Exhibit 2-8 shows the impact of price control on Industry A. When demand shifts out from D to D_1 in the absence of price control, the product price rises from P to P_1. This rise induces an increase in the quantity supplied in the short run from Q_S to Q_1. If the government imposes a legal ceiling price P, then the quantity supplied remains at Q_S; it is not profitable for suppliers to expand output. At P, however, consumers now want to buy Q_D, which exceeds Q_S. The result is a shortage, equal to Q_D minus Q_S.

A surplus can also be a chronic condition if the government fixes a price that is higher than the equilibrium price because it feels that the producers are not getting a fair share. Such surpluses have occurred with several agricultural products. In this case, producers continue to supply more goods than consumers are willing to buy. Again, the artificial restraint obstructs the market's efficient allocation of resources. For example, with a government-established *support price* for wheat, the quantity of wheat supplied will exceed the quantity of wheat demanded. This oversupply becomes chronic because the market price cannot perform its equilibrating function. As illustrated in Exhibit 2-9, the market price, P, will be the equilibrium price at which the supply and demand curves intersect. If the government decrees a higher price, P_1, then the producers will be willing to offer Q_1 quantity of output. At P_1, however, the consumers would want to purchase only Q_2 quantity. Thus the difference between Q_1 and Q_2 is the oversupply, and it is a chronic condition because the price of wheat cannot fall to equilibrate the quantity of wheat supplied and the quantity of wheat demanded.

MARKET CHANGES

Because supply and demand conditions are always changing, markets are constantly in flux. Any change in supply or demand leads to a new market equilibrium. We must distinguish, however, between a

Exhibit 2-8
Impact of Price Control

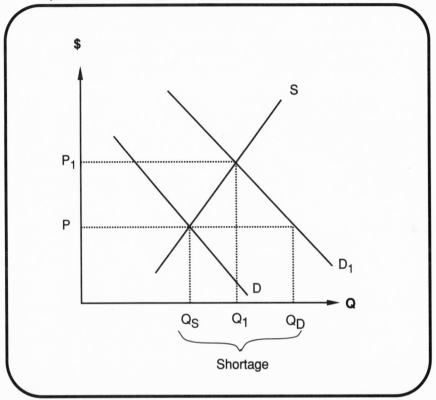

movement along a curve and a shift of a curve. Exhibit 2-10 illustrates this distinction.

Case I shows a change in demand from yesterday to today. Yesterday's demand appears as curve D_1. The curve D_2 represents an *increase* in demand from D_1 because at the same price of P_1, consumers are willing to buy more today (Q_2) than they were yesterday (Q_1). Alternatively, suppose that yesterday the price was P_1 and today's price is P_2. Q_1 was the quantity demanded yesterday and Q_2 is the quantity demanded today as shown in Case II. The quantity Q_2 is larger than Q_1. Both Q_1 and Q_2 are measured from the same demand curve in relation to P_1 and P_2. In both Cases I and II, consumers are willing to buy more, but the reasons are not the same.

In Case I, the price has *not* changed, but consumers are willing to buy more because the demand curve itself has shifted upward. This shift in the demand curve could have resulted from any of those factors discussed—tastes and preferences, income and wealth, prices of other

Exhibit 2-9
Impact of Price Support

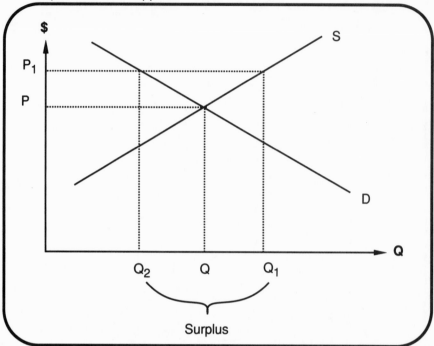

goods, price expectations, or the number of consumers. In Case II the demand curve has remained the same, but the price has changed. None of the factors determining demand has changed, and the change in quantity demanded resulted from the change in price of the product. The change in Case I is signified by a shift in the demand curve. The change in Case II is a change in the quantity demanded—a movement along the same demand curve.

The prices of other goods often affect demand for a specific good. These other goods can be either *substitute goods* or *complementary goods*. For example, an increase in the price of beef might increase the demand for chicken because beef and chicken are substitutes. More people will choose chicken because they are less able to afford beef. A change in the price of complementary goods can also affect demand. If tennis rackets drop in price, more people may take up tennis. When people buy tennis rackets to play tennis, the demand for tennis balls also will increase.

The world of economics is full of substitutes. People may regard housing and transportation as distinct and unrelated commodities, but a close examination may show them to be substitutes. For example, moving closer to the place of work may be a viable substitute for commuting from home to work when the cost of transportation increases. When consumers can find such substitutes, they are less willing to accept price increases.

Elasticity and Revenues

The degree of such consumer response to price changes involves the concept of elasticity. The law of demand states that the quantity of a commodity demanded by consumers tends to change in the direction opposite to the price change, other things being equal. But the law does not specify the degree to which a consumer responds to a change in price. The concept of elasticity applies to this sensitivity to a change in price.

Price Elasticity of Demand For any particular commodity, consumer sensitivity to price changes can normally be described as relatively *elastic* demand, relatively *inelastic* demand, or *unitary elastic* demand. Exhibit 2-12 illustrates these three types of demand curves. The degree to which a consumer responds to a change in price may be measured by the *coefficient of the elasticity of demand*. This coefficient is the percentage change in quantity demanded of a product compared to the percentage change in the price of the product. The mathematical formula for the coefficient of elasticity is

$$\frac{\text{Percentage change in quantity demanded}}{\text{Percentage change in price}} = E$$

Exhibit 2-11 presents three different cases of elasticity. Case 1 shows a relatively elastic demand; Case 2 shows a relatively inelastic demand; and Case 3, a unitary elastic demand. The percentages shown illustrate the differences among the three cases. The key to the measure of elasticity, however, lies with the *relative* changes in quantity demand and in price. Exhibit 2-12 illustrates the demand curves for each of these three cases. The demand for necessities (most food like bread and potatoes) tends to be *inelastic*. The demand for luxuries (such as good wine and precious stones) tends to be *elastic*.

There are also two extreme cases of elasticity. The first is *perfectly elastic demand* when consumers are extremely or infinitely sensitive to the price change. For example, if the price goes up, consumers will purchase none of the product. However, if the price remains the same they will purchase all that is available. The opposite case is *perfectly inelastic demand* when consumers buy exactly the same quantity of the product regardless of the price. This may be because the product is required, such as mandatory personal auto insurance, or because the

Exhibit 2-10
A Change in Demand versus a Change in Quantity Demanded

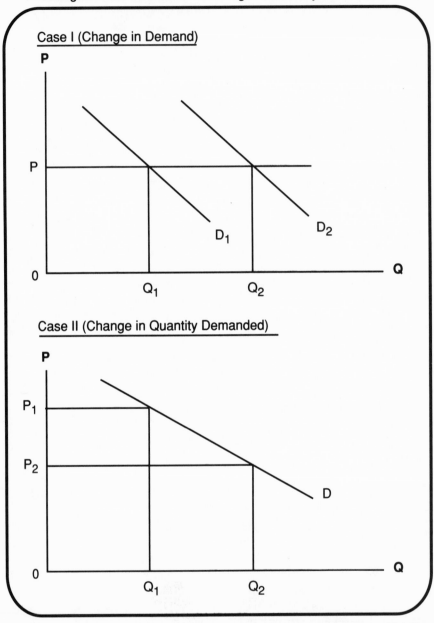

total expenditure on the product is of trivial significance, such as expenditures for salt. Even these examples, however, only approximate perfectly inelastic demand.

Exhibit 2-11
Three Cases of Elasticity

Case	Percentage Change in Price	Percentage Change in Quantity Demanded	Coefficient of Elasticity (e)
1	10%	20%	$\frac{20\%}{10\%} = 2$
2	10%	5%	$\frac{5\%}{10\%} = 0.5$
3	10%	10%	$\frac{10\%}{10\%} = 1$

Over a short time, demand for some necessities with no readily available substitutes may approach perfect inelasticity. In that case the demand curve is nearly vertical. With time, however, the development of substitutes will change the slope of the demand curve as the demand becomes more elastic.

Price Elasticity of Demand Versus Income Elasticity of Demand The preceding examples illustrate the *price elasticity of demand*. This concept relates the change in the quantity demanded to a change in a product's price. In other words, it shows how consumers respond to a price change by adjusting the quantity of the commodity they purchase.

The elasticity concept may also be applied to measuring how consumers respond to a change in income. This measure is the *income elasticity of demand*. It relates the percentage change in a quantity demanded of a product to the percentage change in a consumer's income. As a consumer's income rises, some products become more attractive while others become less attractive. Because the income elasticity of demand measures this effect, it can provide significant marketing information.

Elasticity Along a Given Demand Curve The preceding discussion considered the degree of elasticity implied by one demand curve compared to another. That is, the same percentage increase in price will bring about different percentages of decline in the quantity demanded because of the different elasticities these two demand curves show.

Elasticity also varies along a given demand curve. In one curve there is a range over which there is relative elasticity and another range over which there is relative inelasticity. Exhibit 2-13 presents a demand schedule and a demand curve to illustrate this variation. On this demand curve, when the price drops from $5 to $4 per unit (a 20 percent decline), the quantity demanded rises from one to two units (a 100 percent rise). At the other end of this curve, a 50 percent decline in price from $2 to $1 per unit induces only a 25 percent increase in the quantity demanded. Plugging these numbers into the formula for the coefficient of elasticity yields a coefficient of 5 in the former case (100 percent divided by 20 percent) and a coefficient of 0.5 in the latter (25 percent divided by 50 percent).

Effect of Price Change on Total Revenue The concept of price elasticity is extremely useful in business and government decisionmaking because it gives information about what happens to total revenue when the price of a product changes. *Total revenue* is price times quantity. Price elasticity is intimately related to total revenue because, in general, a price change can affect total revenue in either direction. A decline in price reduces total revenue received from the sale of the same quantity of goods. However, a price cut can also increase total revenue if the price cut stimulates the sale of significantly greater quantities.

If demand is relatively elastic, the quantity demanded increases by a larger percentage than the percentage by which prices drop. In this case, total revenue will increase as price decreases. However, if demand is relatively inelastic, the quantity demanded increases by a smaller percentage than the percentage by which the price declines. Consequently, total revenue decreases as price decreases.

When a firm wants to induce more sales, it can consider lowering the price of its product. If a 10 percent drop in price can generate more than a 10 percent gain in units sold, it might be a good business move. If a 10 percent cut in price can generate a less than 10 percent increase in units sold, then the price cut would not be so good. These examples demonstrate why it is important for businesses to know the price elasticity of demand for their product in the range in which they are operating.

Exhibit 2-14 shows a demand schedule expanded to contain information on total revenue and marginal revenue. *Total revenue* comes from multiplying price by quantity. *Marginal revenue* is the additional or incremental revenue that comes from selling one more unit. Exhibit 2-15 presents this information graphically. In the upper range of prices marginal revenue is positive as a firm sells more when it reduces the price. In the lower range of prices, marginal revenue becomes negative as a firm's sales increase when the price is lowered.

Exhibit 2-12
Three Types of Demand Curves

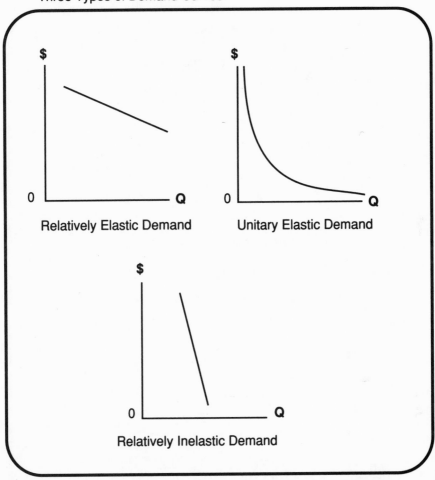

Total revenue also increases at first and then decreases as quantity rises in response to price cuts. Clearly the firm would not wish to lower its price below $5 in an effort to augment sales because after that point it becomes unprofitable.

Long-Run Equilibrium

When any of the underlying economic conditions change, economy-wide adjustments have to be made. The questions *what* to produce, *how* to produce it, and *for whom* should it be produced now require different answers. Dislocations that result from continual shifts in demand and

Exhibit 2-13
Varying Elasticities

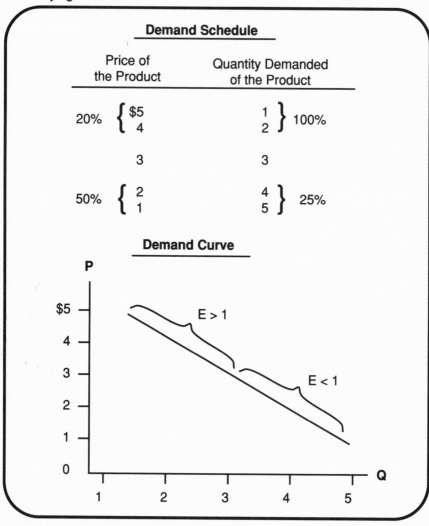

Demand Schedule

Price of the Product		Quantity Demanded of the Product	
20% {	$5	1	} 100%
	4	2	
	3	3	
50% {	2	4	} 25%
	1	5	

Demand Curve

E > 1

E < 1

supply have to be resolved. What a system of competitive markets then accomplishes is almost unbelievably simple.

Without the need to collect large amounts of data spelling out how the availability of resources, consumer preferences, or technology have changed, markets generate the minimum information required and distribute it to those who need it. As changes in underlying parameters translate into shifts in demand or supply curves, potential profits start to change. Commodities falling out of favor with consumers become

Exhibit 2-14
Expanded Demand Schedule

Price of the Product	Quantity Demanded	Total Revenue	Marginal Revenue
$10	1	$10	
9	2	18	$8
8	3	24	6
7	4	28	4
6	5	30	2
5	6	30	0
4	7	28	-2
3	8	24	-4
2	9	18	-6
1	10	10	-8

more difficult to sell, and their prices come under pressure. As prices begin to fall, profits also decline. While owners of affected firms (or their employees) might not like this change, markets reveal in no uncertain terms that their products are not as scarce as they had been and that some of the resources they are using should be redeployed in industries with stronger consumer demand. If there are no artificial barriers to exit, and if consumers can consume less, the appropriate realignment of resources will occur. Of course, both provisions might be violated in noncompetitive markets. For instance, railroads are not free to leave markets where demand for their services has fallen to uneconomically low levels; employers of union workers frequently are not free to substitute more efficient inputs for union labor (feather-bedding and work-rules); and consumers may be obligated by law to continue to consume some commodities for which they have relatively little use.

The same holds when consumer demand for some commodity increases. The initial effect is an increase in the profits of current suppliers. These windfall profits encourage entrepreneurs to increase their output or enter the industry as quickly as they can. If entry is not restricted, these economic profits will draw new resources into the production of commodities that have become relatively more scarce. It is the hope of reaping profits that keeps entrepreneurs actively in

Exhibit 2-15

Marginal Revenue and Total Revenue

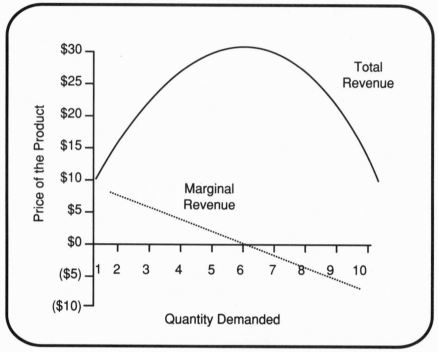

search of ways to serve consumers better and to watch for changes in consumer tastes and preferences. Those who correctly anticipate shifts in consumer demand stand to profit. Those who misread consumer sentiment will lose.

SUMMARY

The fundamental decisions in organizing the economy require the allocation of scarce resources to the most productive uses according to society's needs and wants. A free-market economy allocates resources efficiently because people continually strive to maximize their wealth through rational choices. The market balances people's demand for goods and services against the supply that nature and society make available.

These concepts of supply and demand relate behavior in the market to prices. The demand curve shows the quantity that buyers of a particular commodity are willing and able to purchase at various price levels. The supply curve shows the quantity that sellers of the commodity will offer for sale at various price levels. The intersection of these two curves represents the equilibrium price, where the quantity demanded equals the quantity supplied, thus clearing the market. Because there are few completely free markets, shortages and surpluses sometimes develop when interference prevents the price from reaching its equilibrium level.

The concept of elasticity of demand relates the effect of a change in price on the quantity demanded. Whether the demand for a product is relatively elastic or relatively inelastic is a fundamental concern in the pricing decisions of business firms. Whether their total revenues rise or fall as a result of price changes depends on the elasticity of demand.

Since competitive markets generate flexible signals (prices) of relative scarcity and simultaneously provide compelling motivation (profits and losses) for decisionmakers to heed those signals, they obviate the need for overt, comprehensive planning. Markets, when they work well, are an efficient coordinating and planning mechanism. These adjustments to market signals continually reallocate resources according to consumer preferences. This is the process that Adam Smith described as an invisible hand. Each individual seeks his own enlightened self-interest, but the outcome is an efficient allocation of society's resources overall.

Chapter Note

1. Adam Smith, *The Wealth of Nations* (New York: The Modern Library, 1937), p. 423.

CHAPTER 3

Output and Pricing Decisions

INTRODUCTION

In order to produce goods and services, a business needs certain resources or factors of production. In general, they are *land, labor,* and *capital.* These *factors of production* must be organized in some fashion in a productive unit such as a farm, a factory, a store, or an office. The entrepreneur who organizes these resources to make them productive faces several essential decisions in the process. To maximize profits, the entrepreneur must compare the costs and benefits of operating at various levels of production. When different methods allow the production of a product using different proportions of the required factors, the entrepreneur must also choose the most efficient method. Finally, the entrepreneur must decide how much of the product to make and what price to charge for it.

While decisions regarding the scale and method of production depend largely on relative costs, output and pricing decisions are also influenced by the demand for the product. Thus the structure of the market in which the product is sold is still another variable in these decisions. If the structure allows a firm some market power, the firm chooses different output and pricing than it would in a perfectly competitive market.

THE GOAL OF PROFIT MAXIMIZATION

The goal of most entrepreneurs is to earn the greatest possible profit. In order to choose the most profitable of the available alternatives, an entrepreneur must consider both production costs and

51

revenues involved in each alternative. A firm maximizes its profit when the cost of one additional unit equals the revenue generated by that additional unit. To maintain this equality, a firm adjusts its input and output levels in both the short run and in the long run.

Costs, Revenues, and Profits

Business firms exist to produce and sell products or services that consumers are willing to buy. In considering how much output to produce and how much to charge for each unit of output, the firm needs to know how much it costs to produce and how much revenue it can expect to receive for the output.

Production Costs Production costs involve several different concepts of costs. Decisionmakers need to analyze their costs both in the aggregate and per unit. They also need to analyze their changing costs "at the margin"; in other words, on an incremental basis.

Total Cost. The total cost of production involves two kinds of costs. *Fixed cost* is the cost of production a firm has to pay regardless of its level of output. These costs exist even when the firm's output is zero. The cost for the firm's building and the cost for its machinery and equipment are examples of fixed costs. Any cost is fixed as long as it does not change with the level of output. For example, a firm's cost to acquire or to rent a building for its factory or premises is the same regardless of whether the firm produces and sells one unit or one hundred units or one thousand units—any level of output up to its maximum capacity. The same reasoning applies to the machines and equipment the firm has to employ.

Variable cost is the cost a firm pays as it is producing output. When the firm's output is zero, its variable costs are zero. The costs for raw materials and labor used in production are examples of variable costs. Any cost that changes with the level of output is a variable cost. For example, a publishing company needs to buy more paper in order to produce more copies of the same book.

Total cost is the sum of fixed and variable costs for producing a given level of output.

Unit Cost. A firm's decisionmakers must also consider cost on a per-unit basis. The per-unit basis reveals the effect of the output level because it relates cost to the number of units produced.

Average fixed cost is the fixed cost per unit of output. It is obtained by dividing the fixed cost by the number of units produced. For example, if the fixed cost is $100, then the average fixed cost will be $50 if the firm produces two units in a given period of time. Its average fixed cost will be $10 if it is producing ten units in a given period of time. *Average variable cost* is the variable cost per unit of output. If the variable cost is $500 when ten units are being produced, then the average variable cost is $50. *Average total cost* is the average cost of production per unit of output. It is the sum of average fixed cost and average variable cost.

Marginal Cost. Another important concept is called the *marginal cost.* The marginal cost is the additional or incremental cost of producing one more unit of output. Exhibit 3-1 presents a table of cost and revenue data for a hypothetical firm at various levels of output from zero to fifteen units.

For example, if the firm has already produced eleven units, the marginal cost of increasing the quantity by one more unit would be $87. That cost is the difference between the total cost for eleven units ($661) and the total cost for twelve units ($748). To emphasize that each marginal cost is the difference between two total costs in a row, the table shows each marginal cost on a line between the two total costs.

Revenues The firm's other key consideration is how much revenue it obtains for its output. Exhibit 3-2 adds revenue data at various levels of output from zero to fifteen units to the cost data for the hypothetical firm presented in Exhibit 3-1.

As with costs, there are several important concepts related to revenue. *Total revenue* is the revenue from the sale of a given quantity of output. *Average revenue* is the revenue per unit of output. *Marginal revenue* is analogous to the concept of marginal cost. Just as marginal cost is the increase in total cost when the quantity produced is increased by one unit, so marginal revenue is the increase in total revenue from the sale of the extra unit of output. For example, if the firm has already sold three units, the marginal revenue from selling one more unit (that is, the fourth unit) is the difference between the total revenue when three units are sold and the total revenue when four units are sold. In Exhibit 3-2, that figure is $180. This amount is obtained by subtracting the total revenue at three units ($660) from the total revenue at four units ($840). To emphasize that each marginal revenue is the difference between two sequential total revenues, the table shows each marginal revenue on a line between the two total revenues.

Profit Maximization Profit maximization involves a comparison of total cost to total revenue at various possible levels of output. A firm can decide what quantity to produce by making this comparison of costs and revenues at successive increments of production. The firm must observe how its costs and revenues vary with its output. The rule for profit maximization follows from the comparison of marginal cost and marginal revenue. Marginal cost is the cost for producing one more unit

Exhibit 3-1

Cost and Revenue Data for a Hypothetical Firm

Quantity	Fixed Cost	Variable Cost	Total Cost	Average Fixed Cost†	Average Variable Cost†	Average Total Cost†	Marginal Cost†
0	$100	$ 0	$ 100	—	—	—	
1	100	131	231	$100	131	$231	$131
2	100	228	328	50	114	164	97
3	100	297	397	33	99	132	69
4	100	344	444	25	86	111	47
5	100	375	475	20	75	95	31
6	100	396	496	17	66	83	21
7	100	413	513	14	59	73	17
8	100	432	532	13	54	67	19
9	100	459	559	11	51	62	27
10	100	500	600	10	50	60	41
11	100	561	661	9	51	60	61
12	100	648	748	8	54	62	87
13	100	767	867	8	59	67	119
14	100	924	1,024	7	66	73	157
15	100	1,125	1,225	7	75	82	201

Cost data in this table (and also in Exhibit 3-2) are derived from the following cost equation (production function):

Total cost = $Q^3 - 20 Q^2 + 150 Q + 100$

Thus if Q = 1, then TC = $231; if Q = 10, TC = $600; if Q = 15, TC = $1,225.

†Some figures for average fixed cost, average variable cost, average total cost, and marginal cost are rounded to the nearest dollar.

of output. Marginal revenue is the revenue that one more unit of output yields. If the cost of producing one extra unit is less than the revenue from selling it, it will be profitable for the firm to add that unit to production. If, on the other hand, the cost of the additional unit that the firm contemplates producing is greater than the revenue it can generate, it will be unprofitable to produce that additional unit. Therefore, as long as marginal revenue exceeds marginal cost, the firm

Exhibit 3-2

Selected Cost and Revenue Data for the Same Firm

Quantity	Fixed Cost	Total Cost	Average Total Cost†	Marginal Cost†	Price	Total Revenue	Marginal Revenue	Profit
0	$100	$100	—		$250	$0		$–100
1	100	231	$231	$131	240	240	$240	9
2	100	328	164	97	230	460	220	132
3	100	397	132	69	220	660	200	263
4	100	444	111	47	210	840	180	396
5	100	475	95	31	200	1,000	160	525
6	100	496	83	21	190	1,140	140	644
7	100	513	73	17	180	1,260	120	747
8	100	532	67	19	170	1,360	100	828
9	100	559	62	27	160	1,440	80	881
10	100	600	60	41	150	1,500	60	900
11	100	661	60	61	140	1,540	40	879
12	100	748	62	87	130	1,560	20	812
13	100	867	67	119	120	1,560	0	693
14	100	1,024	73	157	110	1,540	–20	516
15	100	1,225	82	201	100	1,500	–40	275

†Some figures for average total cost and marginal cost are rounded to the nearest dollar.

will want to produce more in order to increase its profit. If marginal revenue falls short of marginal cost, however, the firm will decide not to produce more. And when marginal cost equals marginal revenue, the firm will stop producing more.

This method of marginal analysis may be restated using the concept of *marginal profit*. If marginal revenue exceeds marginal cost, the difference may be defined as marginal profit. That is, marginal profit is the profit that comes from one more unit added to production. The figures in Exhibit 3-3 illustrate this concept of marginal profit.

Exhibit 3-3

Illustration of Marginal Profit

Output Level	Marginal Cost	Marginal Revenue	Marginal Profit	Total Profit
0	0	0	0	0
1	$131	$102	$–29	$–29
2	97	102	5	–24
3	69	102	33	9
4	47	102	57	66
5	31	102	71	137
6	21	102	81	218
7	17	102	85	303
8	19	102	83	386
9	27	102	75	461
10	41	102	61	522
11	61	102	41	563
12	87	102	15	578
13	119	102	–17	561
14	157	102	–55	506
15	201	102	–99	407

The column labeled Marginal Profit shows that marginal profit is minus $29 (a negative marginal profit) when the first unit is produced. When the second unit is produced, however, there is a marginal profit of $5. From then on, marginal profit increases from $33 to $57 to $71 to $81, and then to $85 when the seventh unit is produced. Beyond the seventh unit, marginal profit declines from $83 to $75 to $61 to $41 and finally to $15. After that, when the thirteenth unit is produced, there is a negative marginal profit.

The largest marginal profit occurs when the seventh unit is produced; it yields $85 of marginal profit. There may be a temptation to conclude that this is the best situation for the firm because the marginal profit is the largest at that level of output. However, even though the marginal profit declines beginning with the eighth unit, that additional unit still enlarges the total profit by adding $83 to the total profit. The ninth unit adds $75 to the total profit, and the tenth unit adds $61 to the total profit. The eleventh unit adds $41, and even the twelfth unit still adds $15 to the total profit. Although each successive increment of one unit earns less and less marginal profit, the total profit increases until it reaches the highest level of $578 with output level at twelve units. It is only after the twelfth unit, when marginal profit shows negative figures, that the firm's total profit declines. At the level of thirteen units, total profit declines to $561. Thus a profit-maximizing firm continues to increase its output as long as the marginal profit is greater than zero.

Concept of Economic Profit Although the word profit may seem quite familiar, it has a rather special meaning in economics. Normal profit must be distinguished from economic profit. *Normal profit* is a return to the owner for supplying resources. It compensates the owner for the money he invests in the business, for the property he owns and uses in the business, or for the value of his labor that he contributes to the business. Such compensation is therefore a true cost of production. When the business returns to the owner more than this amount, an *economic profit* occurs. The term economic profit describes any return above the amount considered to be the normal profit. It is the presence of economic profit that encourages existing producers to expand output and induces new producers to enter the industry. On the other hand, *economic loss*, which occurs when the owner receives less than the normal profit, causes a firm to reduce output or perhaps to leave the industry. It also discourages new firms from entering this industry.

The concept of economic profit takes into account implicit costs as well as explicit costs. *Explicit costs* are the costs of production a firm pays for those fixed and variable cost items previously mentioned. These are out-of-pocket costs. *Implicit costs* are the costs of production incurred by the owners of the firm when they use their own money or their own time in the business. If they used their own money when they could have earned 10 percent by lending it to someone, then they have forgone the opportunity of earning 10 percent interest on their money. That 10 percent is the implicit cost or the opportunity cost of using their own money in the business. The same reasoning applies to using their own time and talent for their business. Implicit costs, therefore, are measured by forgone earnings. The total cost of doing business, which we may call *economic cost*, is made up of explicit *plus* implicit costs.

To proceed with the analysis of economic profit, we must incorporate one additional concept, *net revenue*. Net revenue results from subtracting explicit costs from total revenue.

If net revenue *exceeds* implicit costs, then there is an economic profit. If net revenue *equals* implicit costs, then there is no economic profit. This is the condition under which the owner earns only normal return; in other words, only normal profit results. If net revenue *is less than* implicit costs, or to put it differently, if net revenue does not cover implicit costs, then the economic profit is negative. In other words, an economic loss results. Often when a corporation divests a subsidiary or business unit, that unit is producing an accounting profit, but an economic loss. Although it covers its explicit costs, its performance is not satisfactory to its owners, who can employ their resources more effectively elsewhere.

Normal return (or normal profit) may be thought of as the going rate of return for one's capital, talent, or skill. It is the compensation that one's money or skill could have earned on the open market. Economic profit is the net revenue earned above the going rate of return, or above the normal profit.

Rise and Fall of Economic Profit   To illustrate how economic profit arises, declines, and disappears in competitive markets, Exhibit 3-4 presents cost and revenue data for a business called Miraculous Restorations, Inc. Our explanation concentrates on two key aspects: (1)comparison between marginal cost and marginal revenue and (2) comparison between marginal wages and marginal revenue product. The first comparison focuses on the product market; the second on the resource market.

Before discussing these two aspects, it is best to clarify several items presented in Exhibit 3-4. Columns (1) and (2) add up to (3) because total cost is the sum of total fixed cost and total variable cost. Column (4) is average cost, and it comes from dividing total cost in (3) by the number of beams. Column (5) is twice the number of beams because total revenue is the product of the number of beams multiplied by the price, which is $2 per beam. Column (6), profit, is the difference between column (5), total revenue, and column (3), total cost. Columns (7) and (9) are the same as price. Column (11), marginal revenue product, is twice as much as column (10), which is marginal physical product, because the price is $2 per beam.

Marginal Cost and Marginal Revenue Comparison.   Exhibit 3-5 graphs the marginal cost and marginal revenue curves for Miraculous Restorations. According to the rule for maximizing profit discussed earlier, the most profitable level of output is 3,350 beams per week because at this level marginal cost is $1.92 and marginal revenue is $2.00, nearly equaling each other. Producing at 3,395 a week, for example, the firm will have a marginal cost of $2.22, which exceeds the marginal revenue of $2.00. Producing at 3,298 per week, however, it will also satisfy the criterion of marginal cost being less than marginal revenue, but stopping production at this level means that the firm will be forgoing some profit it could achieve if it expanded production.

Exhibit 3-4
Cost and Revenue Data for Miraculous Restorations, Inc.

Miraculous Restorations, Inc., is in the salvage business. Miraculous Restorations has just contracted with an insurance company to pay $1,000 per week for salvage rights to a tornado-damaged golf clubhouse, in which only the heavy wood beams are worth salvaging. The only additional cost of salvaging the beams is labor to do the work. Such workers currently are paid $100 a week per worker. The numbers of beams salvaged per week by varying numbers of workers are shown below. The market for such beams is that of price-takers, and the market price is $2 per beam.

No. of Workers	Beams per Week	(1) Total Fixed Cost	(2) Total Variable Cost	(3) Total Cost	(4) Total Revenue	(5) Profit	(6) Average Cost	(7) Average Revenue	(8) Marginal Cost	(9) Marginal Revenue	(10) Marginal Physical Product	(11) Marginal Revenue Product	(12) Marginal Wages
0	0	$ 0	$ 0	$1,000	$ 0	$ 0	$ 0	$0	$ 0	$0	0	$ 0	$ 0
1	100	1,000	100	1,100	200	−900	11.00	2	1.00	2	100	200	100
2	350	1,000	200	1,200	700	−500	3.43	2	.40	2	250	500	100
3	702	1,000	300	1,300	1,404	104	1.85	2	.28	2	352	704	100
4	1,152	1,000	400	1,400	2,304	904	1.22	2	.22	2	450	900	100
5	1,700	1,000	500	1,500	3,400	1,900	.88	2	.18	2	548	1,096	100
6	2,190	1,000	600	1,600	4,380	2,780	.73	2	.20	2	490	980	100
7	2,604	1,000	700	1,700	5,203	3,503	.65	2	.24	2	414	828	100
8	2,908	1,000	800	1,800	5,816	4,016	.62	2	.33	2	304	608	100
9	3,114	1,000	900	1,900	6,228	4,328	.61	2	.49	2	206	412	100
10	3,240	1,000	1,000	2,000	6,480	4,480	.62	2	.79	2	126	252	100
11	3,298	1,000	1,100	2,100	6,596	4,496	.64	2	1.72	2	58	116	100
12	3,350	1,000	1,200	2,200	6,700	4,500	.66	2	1.92	2	52	104	100
13	3,395	1,000	1,300	2,300	6,790	4,490	.68	2	2.22	2	45	90	100

Exhibit 3-5
Profit Maximization for Miraculous Restorations

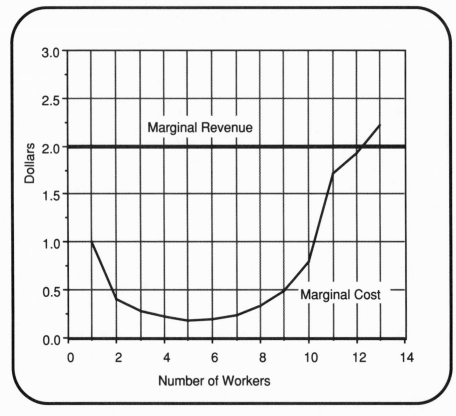

This analysis indicates that the profit-maximizing level of output was 3,350 beams per week. We may wish to consider why the firm was not better off when (1) it produced 1,700 beams per week when marginal cost of $.18 was the lowest of all the marginal costs, or (2) when it produced 3,114 beams per week when the average cost of $.61 was the lowest of all the average costs. In other words, why was the output level that would maximize profit not guided by producing at the lowest marginal cost or at the lowest average cost?

First, even though producing more than 1,700 beams means a rising marginal cost, these marginal costs are still less than marginal revenue of $2.00. If marginal revenue remains the same when marginal cost is rising, as each additional unit is produced, the difference between marginal revenue and marginal cost gets smaller and smaller as the firm increases its level of output until marginal cost nearly equals marginal revenue at 3,350 beams per week. Before that level is reached, every unit the firm produced will add to the profit already accumulated. It may be said that the firm is building a "pyramid of

Exhibit 3-6
The Pyramid of Marginal Profits

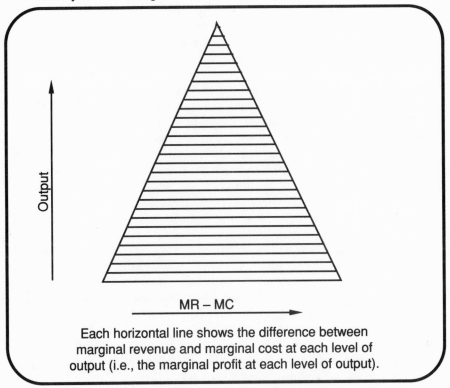

Each horizontal line shows the difference between
marginal revenue and marginal cost at each level of
output (i.e., the marginal profit at each level of output).

marginal profits." Marginal profit, as explained earlier, is the difference
between marginal revenue and marginal cost. When marginal revenue
equals marginal cost at a certain level of output, the firm has reached
the apex of the pyramid, as Exhibit 3-6 shows.

In this diagram the horizontal lines represent the difference
between marginal revenue and marginal cost (marginal profit) at each
different level of output. The pyramid represents the total profit. Even
though the marginal profit shrinks at the higher levels of output, the
total profit is greatest at the top of the pyramid. To maximize profit, the
firm must increase output until it no longer can add any marginal profit
to the profit already made.

Second, even though the lowest average cost is $.61, 3,114 beams a
week is not the output level that will enable the firm to maximize its
profit. Why? As the output increases, although it costs *more* to produce
each beam, the increase in revenue makes it worthwhile for the firm to
produce more. When it increases its output to 3,350 beams from 3,114
beams, its cost goes up by $300, but its revenue rises by $472. When the
average cost is the lowest, the firm is the most efficient, but not
necessarily the most profitable.

Marginal Revenue and Marginal Wage Comparison. In markets for output, consumers express the demand for a particular output in light of their preferences for the product, their income levels, the prices of other commodities, and their expectations about the future price of the product. In markets for inputs, there is likewise the interplay of demand and supply. In this case, demand and supply refer to the demand for factors of production and supply of these factors of production. The concept of demand and supply is still the same, even though applied to different objects. In markets for inputs, the demand for land, labor, and capital, for example, does not originate from the entrepreneur's innate desire to consume such resources. Rather the entrepreneur's demand for land, labor, and capital stems from the desire to use these resources in order to produce the goods and services that the consumers in the product markets would like to have. Therefore, the demand for factors of production is called *derived demand*. Demand in the resource market is derived from the demand for output in the product market.

What determines a firm's demand for factors of production? Suppose we use the example of labor, the most common factor of production. A firm in a competitive market accepts the going market price for its product, and on that basis the firm decides how much output to produce or supply. In order to produce that output, the firm needs to purchase factors of production. As a simplification, we consider only the labor of one particular skill level, although in reality there are many different skill levels of labor, each commanding a different wage, as well as other factors of production.

The firm's decision to produce one more unit is reached by comparing the additional revenue (marginal revenue) to the additional cost (marginal cost). The firm increases its level of output until the point where marginal revenue equals marginal cost. The firm uses the same kind of marginal analysis to decide how many units of labor to hire.

The firms asks: "If we hire another worker, how much will our cost increase? How much will our revenue increase? If the gain in revenue exceeds the increase in cost, we should hire another worker, and ask the question again as to whether we should hire yet one more worker. If not, we should not."

In order to proceed with the analysis at the margin, we need to distinguish two concepts, marginal physical product and marginal revenue product.

The cost of hiring a worker is the wage. What is the additional revenue that results from hiring one more worker? In order to answer this question, we need to take two steps. First, we need to know how much more physical output this additional worker will produce. This increase in physical output is called the *marginal physical product* of labor. Second, we need to know how much more revenue this amount of additional physical output will yield. This gain in revenue can be calculated by multiplying the increase in output by its selling price. This gain in revenue is called the *marginal revenue product.* If one more worker can produce 100 units of physical output and each unit of this output can be sold for $80, then the marginal physical product is 100 units and the marginal revenue product is $8,000.

These concepts enable the firm to compare the marginal revenue and the marginal wage. If the annual going wage for a worker of this skill is $6,000, it would be profitable for the firm to hire this worker. After hiring this worker, the same question should be asked concerning the next worker. As more workers are hired, *diminishing returns* will eventually set in, assuming plant capacity and equipment remain fixed. The marginal physical product of labor declines as additional workers are hired because as more workers are added to the same amount of capital, the contribution to output by each additional worker declines. Even if the selling price of the output remains constant, the marginal revenue product of labor, which equals the marginal physical product of labor times the price of the product, will decline. Thus this firm should hire workers until the marginal revenue product of labor falls to $6,000 (75 units multiplied by $80 per unit of output), the going wage rate for one worker. As more workers are added to a fixed amount of capital, the decline in the marginal physical product of labor can be averted by the infusion of additional capital. In other words, marginal physical product increases as the ratio of capital to labor increases.

Marginal cost is related to marginal wage because wages are an element of cost. Marginal revenue is related to marginal product because sales of the product generate revenue. It is these relationships that make the product market and the factor market interdependent.

Miraculous Restorations, for example, will try to produce at the level that maximizes its profit, 3,350 beams a week. Since it is profit maximizing, the firm sees no reason to change its operation until supply and demand conditions in the market change. It is therefore in a state of no-change or a state of stability, which economists call *equilibrium.* When the firm is in equilibrium, it reaches its best position in the product market by producing 3,350 beams a week; it reaches its best position in the factor market by hiring twelve workers a week.

When hiring twelve workers a week, the marginal wage is $100 and the marginal revenue product is $104. At this point the marginal revenue product is nearly the same as marginal wage. Let us examine, however, the firm's options when the employment level is less than twelve workers. The marginal product is highest when the firm has five workers. As it hires more than five workers, it experiences diminishing returns and rising marginal costs. However, it is still profitable to expand. Suppose the firm is employing eight workers. The eighth worker costs the firm $100, but the eighth worker generates for the firm $608. In other words, Worker 8 adds $100 to the firm's cost, but more than $600 to the firm's revenue. Worker 9 also costs the firm $100, but adds $412 to the firm's revenue. Even though Worker 9 adds less than Worker 8, it pays the firm to hire Worker 9 because otherwise profit would be $312 less. Column (5) of Exhibit 3-4 confirms this reasoning. With eight workers the profit is $4,016. With nine workers the profit is $4,328. If the firm hires thirteen workers instead of twelve, Worker 13 adds $100 to the cost of doing business, but adds only $90 to the firm's revenue. Therefore, as Column (5) shows, when thirteen workers are hired, the profit declines to $4,490 from $4,500 when twelve workers are hired. This information demonstrates that the firm will continue to employ more workers as long as each additional worker's marginal revenue product exceeds the marginal wage. The firm should not hire more workers if the additional worker entails a marginal wage that exceeds the marginal revenue product that worker contributes. Thus the firm must stop hiring when the marginal wage of the worker is equal to the marginal revenue product of that worker.

Input and Output Relationships

Unit costs vary according to the scale of production. An entrepreneur must observe the relationship between input and output at various levels of production in order to have the information needed to make the correct decisions. The previous examples presented this information as given. We now consider the reasons that unit costs vary according to the scale of production.

Short Run Versus Long Run Adjustments At the outset, however, we should clarify the distinction between short-run and long-run adjustments. The *short run* is a period in which a firm can increase or decrease its output only by changing its variable costs. In the short run, fixed costs are indeed fixed. The *long run* is a period in which a firm can increase or decrease its output by not only changing its variable costs elements but also its fixed cost elements.

In other words, short run and long run are not defined periods of time in the usual sense; they are relative concepts. It may be that the long run in one industry is shorter than the short run in another industry. For example, a corner grocery store makes a long-run adjustment when it adds refrigeration equipment that can be acquired within a few months. On the other hand, the short run for a railroad may involve years because it needs that much time to change fixed cost elements such as railroad tracks.

Profit-maximizing firms make both short-run and long-run adjustments in an effort to operate at the optimal level. At different output levels, the marginal product varies as the firm experiences either increasing or diminishing returns. The firm's average cost per unit also varies at different output levels, depending on whether there are economies of scale.

Economies of Scale A firm's average costs involve the relationship between cost per unit and volume of output. If a firm faces substantial fixed costs in the short run, in the long run it can reduce its average cost per unit of output by expanding the number of units it produces. This phenomenon is called an *economy of scale.*

By definition, an alteration of the firm's capacity is a long-run adjustment. In the long run, the firm can use whatever inputs it wants. If market conditions warrant, it can operate with greater or smaller capacity. None of its inputs are fixed. Costs of production, of course, depend on the scale at which the firm chooses to operate. The larger the operation, the more it can employ specialized personnel and equipment. Since they are likely to be more productive than generalists, we can expect average costs to decline. This reduction of average costs is an economy of scale.

It is difficult to overestimate the importance of economies of scale. It is because of economies of scale that it becomes profitable to organize production in the form of business firms. Without economies of scale, it would not matter whether output were produced at small or at large levels. Each of us could provide for all our own needs by producing everything ourselves. We could build our own cars, refine our own gasoline, make our own clothes, and produce whatever else we needed. Because there are significant economies of scale in all these production processes, however, we could never hope to do so at the same cost as the businesses that have specialized in their production. As long as the resource cost per unit of output can be reduced by increasing output levels, specialization and mass production will expand the production and consumption possibilities of society.

Economies of scale are particularly important for financial institutions like banks and insurance companies. Their business involves highly specialized processing of transactions. Underwriting an insurance policy, for example, requires expert judgment. Since a specialist can make better underwriting decisions than a generalist, insurance companies employ underwriting specialists. The more policies an underwriter processes, the lower the average cost. The possibility of such economies of scale drives many business firms to expand operations to a more efficient level.

The Choice of Production Methods

Profit-maximizing firms strive to operate efficiently. Economic efficiency means using the lowest cost production technique. The cost of any particular production technique can be determined by adding together the costs of the inputs it requires.

Suppose there are four alternative methods for producing 100 units of a product per month. These methods require different amounts of capital and labor as follows:

Method	Capital Required	Labor Required
A	6 units	200 units
B	40 units	50 units
C	10 units	150 units
D	10 units	250 units

Which method should be used? All four methods can produce 100 units of the product, but they result in different costs. Method D can be rejected because it uses the same amount of capital as does method C, but more labor. Thus Method D is obviously more costly than method C, and therefore less economically efficient. To choose the most efficient of method from among A, B, and C, however, we must have the relevant cost data. Let us assume that three different cost conditions could exist.

Cost Conditions	—Per Unit Cost of—	
	Capital	Labor
I	$50	$3
II	20	5
III	15	5

Then, the comparative costs of Methods A, B, and C are the following:

Cost Conditions	A	B	C
I	$ 900	$2,150	$950
II	1,120	1,050	950
III	1,090	850	950

Therefore, the least cost or the most efficient method depends on cost conditions. Under Cost Condition I, Method A is the best; under Cost Condition II, Method C is the best; under Cost Condition III, Method B is the best. The most economically efficient method of production depends on the relative costs of labor versus capital.

There are some interesting and useful implications from this illustrative discussion. Suppose we employ Method A because it results in the least cost of production as compared with other methods. That is, we have Cost Condition I. If the cost condition changes to that of II, our method is no longer the best (that is, the least cost). We will want to switch to some other method of production.

Changing conditions of resource availability can change the relative cost of labor and capital. These changes in relative costs of inputs may require changes in the methods of production, which mean changes in the use of different resources. The development of new technology can lead to new production methods that may even use different resources to produce the same product.

Economic profits act as spurs to technological change. While the ability to increase price in response to increased demand is one way of increasing profits, reducing costs of production also increases profits. And since maximum profits in the long run are zero, there is a positive incentive for entrepreneurs to try to create disequilibrium by searching for cost-reducing techniques. Such activity frees resources for other uses and essentially shifts society's production possibilities frontier outward.

For example, the Industrial Revolution may be viewed as a process of coping with the resource constraints that began to constrict economic growth. In England wood was once used for a number of purposes such as building material, fuel, and chemical inputs. During the reign of Queen Elizabeth I, wood fuel prices rose about three times as rapidly as general prices. In the early seventeenth century, timber supplies were being depleted, and laws were passed to limit forging and furnace operations in areas where timber became increasingly scarce. In time, however, the Industrial Revolution substituted coal for wood as a source of fuel and power, and builders learned to use abundant iron in place of timber. The changeover was long in coming because until technological problems were solved, using coal instead of wood in glass making, baking, and iron production resulted in inferior products.

Due to abundant timber resources, the United States developed extensive technology in wood-working machinery, which by the 1850s was the most advanced in the world. The large fireplaces in early American homes illustrate the lavish use of an abundant resource, since they were designed to burn large logs that were no longer available in Europe. Similarly, while the American builder used wood, the European builder used stone or iron. Americans also used wood to construct bridges, aqueducts, and even roads.

In the middle nineteenth century timber prices began to rise. As a result, a shift toward coal occurred, in some cases rather rapidly. For example, at the beginning of the Civil War, cord wood supplied the energy needs of the railroads, but twenty years later, railroads were using twenty times as much coal as wood.

These examples show that as the relative price of the resource currently in use increases, other resources become more economically attractive alternatives. Technology develops to exploit these abundant and relatively inexpensive alternative resources. Entrepreneurs apply the new technology to find new production methods with lower costs than the method that had once seemed the best choice.

The Most Profitable Level of Output

A profit-maximizing firm thus faces many choices en route to determining its most profitable level of output. By adjusting its variable inputs in the short run and its production methods in the long run, it seeks to increase its profits. However, the most profitable level of output may not be the most efficient. How can the most efficient level of output not be at the same time the most profitable level of output for a firm? After all, the most efficient level of output is judged by the least cost of production. Here is the answer to the mystery.

Exhibit 3-7 illustrates the relationship between the average cost and the marginal cost of production. This diagram has q_1, q_2, and q_3 on the output axis. The point q_1 denotes 100 units of the product when the average cost of producing those 100 units is being measured; q_1 also denotes the 100th unit of the product when a marginal cost of producing the 100th unit is being measured. Likewise, q_2 shows 200 units when average costs of producing 200 units are being measured; it also shows the 200th unit when the marginal cost of producing the 200th unit is being measured. The same reasoning applies to q_3.

At q_1 each unit costs $1.10 ($AC_1$). Also at q_1 the 100th unit costs $.60 ($MC_1$).

At q_2, each unit in the 200 units costs $1.00 ($AC_2$). At q_2 the 200th unit costs $1.00 ($MC_2$).

At q_3, the average cost of producing 300 units is $1.20, and the 300th unit costs $1.80.

Now the question: at what output level will the firm maximize its profit? The answer depends on what marginal revenue is. If marginal revenue equals $1.00, then q_2 is the output that maximizes its profit. But if marginal revenue is $1.80, the profit-maximizing output is q_3.

When is the most efficient level of output (that is, the least-cost output level) also the most profitable level of output? The diagram in Exhibit 3-8 shows the answer.

At P_1, q_1 is the most profitable *as well as* the most efficient level of output because here $MC = MR_1$. At the price of P_1, quantity q_1 satisfies the condition of marginal cost equaling marginal revenue to yield the maximum amount of profit; it also fulfills the criterion that the average cost for producing q_1 level of output is at the lowest among average costs at other levels of output.

At price level P_2, q_1 remains the most efficient level of output because q_1 quantity of output is being produced at the lowest average cost possible. However, it is not the most profitable level of output, as q_2 is now the most profitable level of output because it meets the condition of equality between MC and MR_2. The shaded area shows the profit.

Exhibit 3-7
Average Cost and Marginal Cost

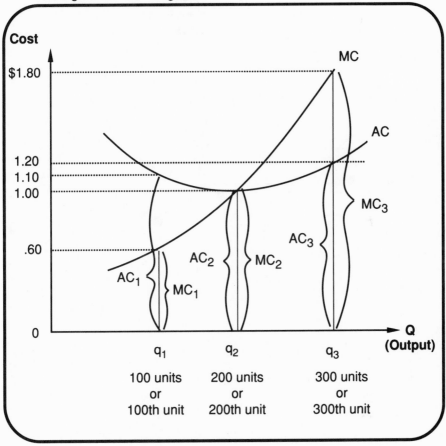

THE EFFECT OF MARKET STRUCTURE ON
OUTPUT AND PRICING DECISIONS

While decisions regarding scale and production methods depend on the cost of various factors, output and pricing decisions also depend on the structure of the market for the product. Economists use the word "market" to refer to all kinds of circumstances under which exchanges (sales and purchases) take place. A market can be, but is not necessarily, a physical location in which such exchanges occur. Markets can include transactions involving a particular commodity or service that are made by telephone or telegram. For example, a local supermarket in which milk, bread, vegetables, fruits, and meats are

Exhibit 3-8

Average Cost, Marginal Cost, and Marginal Revenue

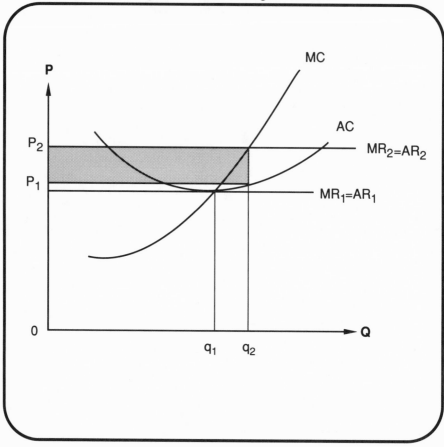

sold is, of course, a market, but sales and purchases of stock and bonds by electronic means in different parts of the country also constitute a market.

Types of Market Structures

Economists conventionally classify product markets according to (1) how many firms are involved, (2) whether these firms are selling the same or different product, and (3) whether or not there is freedom of entry into the market. These considerations conventionally lead to the delineation of four types of markets: perfect competition, pure monopoly, monopolistic competition, and oligopoly.

Perfect Competition Perfect competition is a market characterized by many sellers of the same product with each seller so small that no individual seller has any effect on the prevailing price for the product. That is, each seller supplies such a small portion of the total market that withholding or reducing that output for sale does not affect the market price. This type of market can be closely approximated in agricultural products. The sellers in this market supply an identical product, such as wheat or corn of a given grade. Because the product is identical, it makes no difference whether the consumer buys it from farmer A or farmer B.

In this type of market there is also freedom of entry. That is, there are no artificial restrictions on who may enter the market to produce the product. In other words, no restriction is imposed by the government or by any organized producer groups.

Perfect competition also means that all the participants in the market have complete information. All buyers, for example, know the qualities and the limitations of the product, and all sellers have equal access to market information. Thus buyers compete with one another on equal terms, and sellers do likewise.

Although perfect competition is one of the conventional types of market structure, economists do not argue that it exists in the real world, nor that it has ever existed in its pure form. The reason that perfect competition is studied as a market structure is that it furnishes a simple model or norm against which the performance of other markets may be evaluated.

Pure Monopoly A market structure diametrically opposed to perfect competition is called pure monopoly. In this type of market, there is only one seller providing a unique product. Such a market may involve considerable barriers to entry. Public utilities such as city water, electricity, and local transit systems are examples of pure monopolies.

Monopolistic Competition Like perfect competition, the market structure known as monopolistic competition involves many producers and sellers. However, they sell different products. The difference in the product may be real or imagined. In other words, restaurant A and restaurant B may both sell hamburgers, but in the eyes of consumers, the hamburgers from these two restaurants seem different, or there may be real differences in the hamburgers. In such a market structure, there may be minor barriers to entry. Most retail businesses are examples of monopolistic competition.

Oligopoly The type of market structure called oligopoly comprises only very few producers and sellers. They may produce identical products such as aluminum or steel, or they may produce different products such as automobiles. In this type of market structure, there are usually considerable barriers to entry.

Market Power

The most significant characteristic of any particular market is the degree of market power exercised by the participants. Market power is the ability of a single market participant to influence the price of the product. This characteristic determines whether producers are price-takers or price-searchers.

Price-Takers In perfectly competitive markets, all participants are price-takers. A price-taker is a producer or seller who must "take" the price for the product that is determined in the market for that product. The price-taker firm is so small relative to the market as a whole that each firm's output decision has no appreciable effect on the market because its output constitutes such an imperceptibly small part of the total. This does not mean that a price-taker firm must be very small in terms of value of assets, output, or sale. A wheat farm in the United States can be very large in terms of land area, value of capital equipment, and annual output. However, even the largest farm produces only a very small portion of the total wheat supply in the country. If a large wheat farmer doubles output, or halves it, neither action has any effect on the price of wheat as determined in the market.

Since a price-taker's market is one in which there are many producers of an identical product, the demand curve for the product as seen by the producer or the price-taker firm is a perfectly elastic one, as Exhibit 3-9 illustrates.

The horizontal demand curve is the demand curve facing a price-taker, or any firm in a perfectly competitive industry. To put it differently, a horizontal demand curve is the demand curve as seen by the firm. The firm "takes" the going price as determined in the marketplace. Such a demand curve exists when the consumer will buy all there is to be bought (or offered for sale by the firm) at the going price, p in the diagram, but will go to its competitors if the firm raises the price to p_1, for example. (The demand curve at p_1 is represented by a broken line, meaning that there is no demand at this price.) Because the products are identical, it makes no difference whether the consumer buys from farmer A or from farmer B. Thus the lowest price prevails.

Price-Searchers On the other hand, a price-searcher operates in a market (whether pure monopoly, monopolistic competition, or oligopoly) where the firm has a certain amount of influence over the price of its product or the quantity of its products sold (but not both). Often a price-searcher sells a unique or differentiated product. For example, monopo-

Exhibit 3-9
The Demand Curve as Seen by the Price-Taker

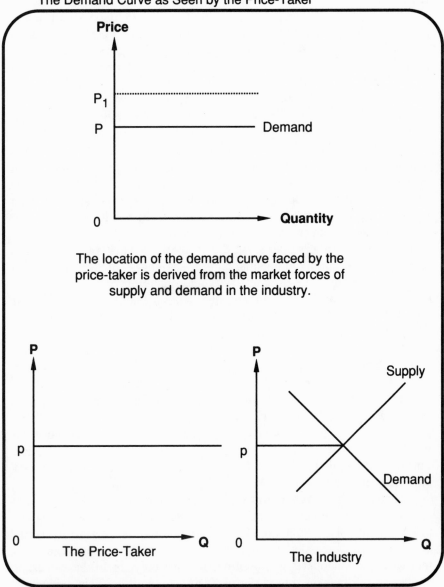

The location of the demand curve faced by the price-taker is derived from the market forces of supply and demand in the industry.

listic competition exists in a wide range of businesses such as gasoline stations, grocery stores, beauty salons, restaurants, clothiers, cleaners, and various retail outlets. If there are many competing producers or firms, there is some differentiation in the product or service each offers. Because of the uniqueness of the product, a price-searcher enjoys a certain amount of loyalty from its customers. They cannot readily buy from someone else without some sacrifice.

Price-searchers can also be found in an industry with many producers, but where imperfect competition prevails, perhaps because of information problems. For example, price-searchers may sell toothpaste or detergents that are essentially the same products, but that still differ in the minds of consumers.

Some products such as steel or aluminum are not unique, but relatively few firms supply them. In the automobile industry, there are both differentiated products and few suppliers. The steel, aluminum, and automobile industries are conventionally considered oligopolistic industries. The economies of scale in these industries create significant barriers to entry for new firms. A price-searcher can also be a single producer selling a product or service without close substitutes. This monopoly situation often exists for public utilities. Sometimes these monopolies are even created by legal barriers.

While price-takers operate in the competitive markets at the mercy of the forces of supply and demand, price-searchers frequently strive to build demand for their products without competing in price. Advertising can offer marketing advantages. The marketing strategies of monopoly firms, for example, often emphasize community service and institutional public relations advertising.

While a price-taker has no control over the price determined in the marketplace by the forces of supply and demand, a price-searcher may affect the market price when it reduces or increases its output. In oligopoly and monopolistic competition the price-searcher has some influence or control over market price because of the following that the producer may be able to claim among consumers. In a pure monopoly a price-searcher may have a considerable degree of control over price, unless regulated by a utilities commission or other government authority that maintains a certain reasonable level of prices.

Thus a price-searcher firm faces a demand curve that is downward sloping because some of its customers continue to buy even at higher prices. Exhibit 3-10 illustrates the demand curve facing a price-searcher. The downward-sloping demand curve applies in all cases of monopoly, monopolistic competition, or oligopoly; in other words, it applies in any market that is not perfectly competitive. This distinction between price-takers and price-searchers reflects the slope of the demand curve. For a price-taker there is a horizontal demand curve; for a price-searcher there is a downward-sloping demand curve.

Exhibit 3-10
The Demand Curve Faced by the Price-Searcher Is
Downward-Sloping

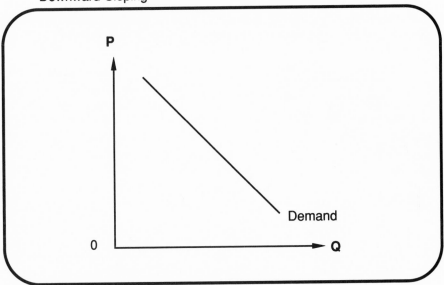

Output and Pricing Decisions: Price-Takers Versus Price-Searchers

This difference in the shape of the demand curve facing price-takers and price-searchers explains the difference in their output and pricing decisions. While a price-taker can never earn an economic profit in the long run, the downward-sloping demand curve gives price-searchers an opportunity to earn economic profits.

Profit for Price-Takers The output and pricing decisions of price-takers may be understood with the aid of the three diagrams in Exhibit 3-11. Diagram 1 shows two corresponding graphs. The graph on the left indicates the price in the industry determined by the given supply and demand schedules. This price, p, is taken by the price-taker. The graph on the right shows the demand curve as seen by the price-taker. This horizontal line is at once the demand curve faced by the firm, the average revenue (AR); and the marginal revenue (MR).

The graph on the right in Diagram 2 shows the marginal cost and average cost curves along with the marginal revenue and average revenue lines. Since the firm tries to maximize its profit, the level of output that the price-taker is expected to produce is q_1, the point that

Exhibit 3-11
Normal Profit for a Price-Taker

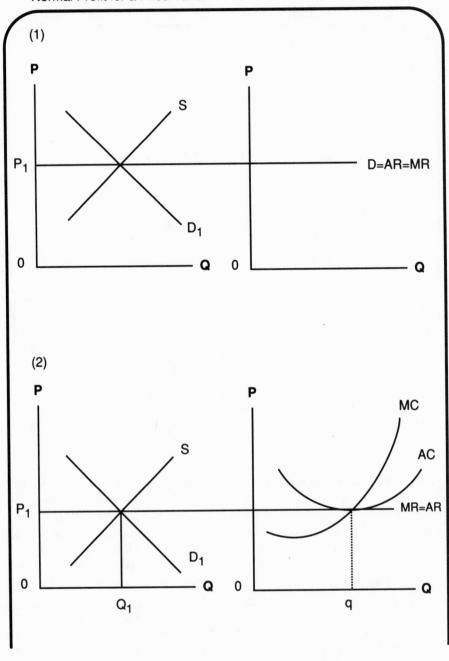

Exhibit 3-11, Continued

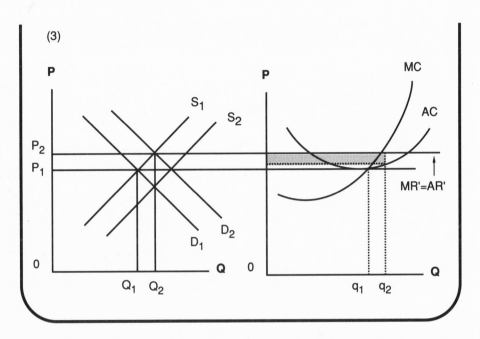

equates marginal cost with marginal revenue. The total output in the industry then is denoted as Q_1 in the graph on the right.

If the total demand for the product in the industry increases from D_1 to D_2, then the price in the industry will move up from p_1 to p_2 as shown in Diagram 3. This new price, p_2, is taken by the price-taker. This higher price for the product results in a new marginal revenue, MR, and a new average revenue, AR. The price-taker will be producing a larger output at q_2. The shaded area in the graph on the right represents an economic profit enjoyed by the price-taker.

The economic profit can only be a transient or short-run phenomenon, however, as it will be competed away in the long run. Since each price-taker is increasing its output from q_1 to q_2, the supply in the industry will soon increase. The increase in the total output will carry with it increases in the prices of resources needed to increase the supply. Because firms need more of these resources in order to expand the supply, they will have to pay higher prices for them. As a result, the cost curve will move up. As the cost curve moves up, the area for economic profit (the rectangular area) becomes smaller. This is the tendency for economic profit to be competed away.

Another force in the market also will tend to reduce the economic profit. More firms are attracted into the business because of that economic profit. As more firms enter the industry, the supply curve will shift to the right from S_1 to S_2. When this happens, the equilibrium price for this product will be driven down from p_2 back to p_1.

As a matter of fact, the market or the industry may indeed experience an oversupply in the sense of too much increase in the supply of the product. This can happen either because existing firms are raising their output level too much or because there are too many new firms coming into the market. In either case, it is possible that the greatly increased supply could drive the market price below the level where it was before the increase in demand. A lower price can cause an economic loss instead of economic profit. Such losses provide a potent force to drive out some firms from the industry or make remaining firms cut their scale of operation. The result of these cutbacks is to move the supply curve to the left, reflecting a reduction in supply.

These possibilities demonstrate a price-taker's adjustments to changes in demand. The output and pricing decisions of all firms in the industry lead toward an equilibrium in which there is neither an economic profit nor an economic loss for the typical firm.

Profit for Price-Searchers Because of its market power, a price-searcher might seem destined to enjoy economic profit. However, a price-searcher can set one of the two variables, price of the product or the quantity of the product sold, but not both. Therefore, even a price-searcher can suffer losses when costs increase.

As Exhibit 3-12 indicates, depending on the relationship of costs and revenues, a price-searcher may be making economic profit or only the normal profit, or it may be suffering losses. Diagram (a) shows the price-searcher making an economic profit because the average revenue, AR, exceeds average cost, AC, for each unit sold. The difference between AR and AC is indicated by the distance between A and B. In other words, AQ_1 is the average revenue and BQ_1 is the average cost. Since OQ_1 is the total number of units sold, AB multiplied by OQ_1 gives the total amount of the profit gained, which is shown by the shaded rectangle.

Diagram (b) shows a price-searcher making only a normal profit. At the total quantity sold of OQ_1, average revenue and average cost are equal. Thus the price each unit brings is just enough to cover the average cost of producing each unit at that level of output.

Diagram (c) shows a price-searcher operating at a loss. This loss occurs because the average cost of producing each unit at the Q_1 level of output is greater than the average revenue at this level of output. The difference between AC and AR multiplied by the quantity produced

Exhibit 3-12
Economic Profit, Normal Profit, or Economic Losses:
The Price-Searcher

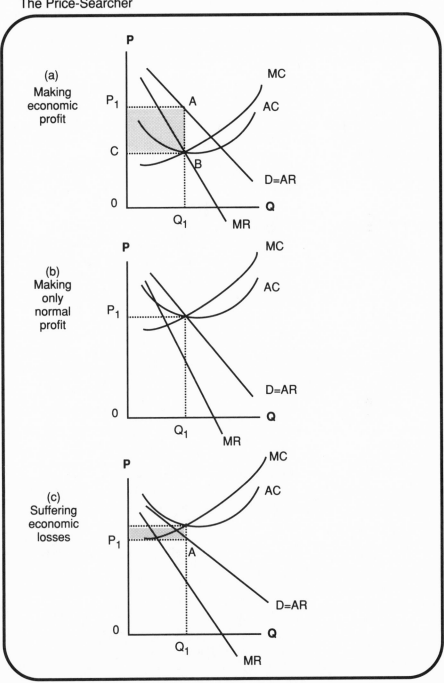

Exhibit 3-13

Long-Run Adjustment for a Price-Searcher

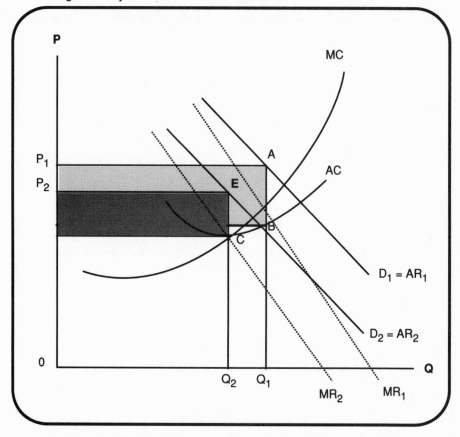

equals the amount of the loss. In this diagram the shaded rectangle represents the amount of the loss.

Even when a price-searcher is making an economic profit, it will not necessarily last. Exhibit 3-13 shows the long-run adjustment for a price-searcher when the level of demand changes. At the P_1 level of price and Q_1 level of output, the price-searcher is making an economic profit as measured by the lighter shaded rectangle. This amount of economic profit will fall if the demand for product declines from D_1 to D_2. At the D_2 level of demand, average revenue drops from AQ_1 to EQ_2, and average cost drops from BQ_1 to CQ_2. The lighter rectangle is the economic profit at Q_1 level of output. The darker rectangle is the economic profit at Q_2 level of output. The latter is a smaller area than the former, which shows that the economic profit declines when demand falls.

If the price-searcher is operating at the P_2 level of price and Q_2 level of quantity, an increase in demand from D_2 to D_1 will enlarge the economic profit. In either case, the price-searcher adjusts its output so that it operates at the point where marginal cost equals marginal revenue. By following this rule, it maximizes profits. The same profit-maximizing rule applies to both price-takers and price-searchers, but price-searchers may find maximum profits at a point that is not the lowest average cost. They have no incentive to expand production to the most efficient level, since they may earn higher profits by restricting output and keeping prices high.

SUMMARY

Economic decisionmaking for producers of goods and services means making the most of the possibilities open to them. They choose what to produce, what methods to use, and how much to produce according to which options will bring them the greatest profits.

Profit is the excess of revenues over costs. The total cost of production includes fixed costs and variable costs. Because variable costs depend on the quantity involved, the average cost per unit of output also changes according to the number of units produced. Thus the decision regarding the optimal level of output must be made at the margin. That is, the decisionmaker compares the costs and benefits of one additional unit of output, one unit *at a time*. As long as the marginal revenue exceeds the marginal cost, producing the additional unit will increase profits. A similar comparison enables a decisionmaker to determine whether to hire additional factors of production. For each type of input, whether it is workers or raw materials, as long as the marginal revenue gained from the additional unit of input exceeds the marginal cost of the additional unit, hiring that additional unit will increase profits. These comparisons allow an entrepreneur to adjust the input and output relationships to achieve economies of scale and to produce in the most efficient manner.

The entrepreneur's choice of production methods depends on the relative costs of the various factors of production as well as on the quantity of output resulting from each of the possible methods. Since relative costs can change over time, the most efficient production method can also change. When the cost of one input significantly increases, for example, the entrepreneur may find it more efficient to substitute another factor of production. Increasing energy prices during the 1970s caused many producers to change their production methods. In the same way technological advances often make it possible for entrepreneurs to lower production costs by substituting new machinery for labor.

Output and pricing decisions depend on the structure of the market. A perfectly competitive market includes many buyers and many sellers offering identical products. There are no barriers to entry or exit and everyone has complete information. In this situation a single producer cannot control the price, but must take whatever price prevails in the market. A price-taker, therefore, strives to produce at the lowest possible average cost and adjusts output to maximize profits. In the long run, however, competitors undercut those profits until an equilibrium occurs at which point the price equals the average cost, the marginal cost, and the marginal revenue.

In reality, however, few markets are perfectly competitive. Monopoly, monopolistic competition, and oligopoly are market structures in which producers have some control over either price or output (but never both). Thus they are price-searchers instead of price-takers. They face a downward-sloping demand curve rather than the horizontal demand curve that faces price-takers. Price-searchers also maximize profits by producing at the level where marginal cost equals marginal revenue, but that level is not necessarily the most efficient. The less efficient allocation of resources that results from this degree of market power exercised by price-searchers is one of the issues addressed in the next chapter.

CHAPTER 4

Market Success and Market Failure

INTRODUCTION

One of the most important lessons of economics is that any society must somehow work within the constraints imposed by the ultimate scarcity of resources. The simple and inescapable fact that resources are limited means that the goods and services that determine our standard of living cannot be as abundant as we would like. While we cannot produce enough of all goods and services to satisfy the wants and desires of every individual, we can shift resources and change the mix of goods and services produced. Choices, however, must be made. In order to satisfy particular wants, some other goals and objectives must be at least partially sacrificed.

Society can decide issues such as *what to produce, how to produce,* and *for whom to produce* in numerous ways. Part of the job of economists is to evaluate how such problems of resource allocation are resolved most effectively and to suggest ways of improving the choices actually made. This chapter examines conditions that characterize efficient choices. It also investigates institutional arrangements that make efficient choices more likely.

Evaluating different solutions to allocation problems is difficult, and economists have not been completely successful. One reason is that subjective judgments are required. While nearly everyone would agree that it is better to have society produce more rather than less of all goods and services, the issue is not as clear when we propose to produce more of some but less of others. In particular, when there are both gainers and losers from some proposed change in the economic environment, economic science can provide only limited help in evaluating the total impact of the change. Potential gainers will surely praise the change, while potential losers will object. But who is to say whether society as a whole will benefit from the change? Who is to say whether the gains of the winners will offset the losses of the losers? The issue is so subjective that many economists accept the proposition that objective, scientific answers to the question are not possible given the current state of economic knowledge.

However, in a great many situations economic analysis is extremely useful. Economists can identify some situations where realignments of resources create winners and no losers. It is in these situations that economic analysis investigates whether there are any changes that could be made in the way society is dealing with the fundamental issue of scarcity so as to make at least some individuals better off at the expense of none. The central concept in such analysis is the notion of efficiency.

After we have identified the conditions that characterize efficient solutions, we will compare them to the solutions generated by competitive markets. We will see that under some circumstances the two are the same. This remarkable result, the product of Adam Smith's invisible hand, is the foundation for much of the free market or laissez faire philosophy that pervades contemporary American political, popular, and academic opinion.

After we have studied the conditions under which markets might yield efficient solutions to economic problems, we will look at some of the things that might spoil the results. These fall under the general heading of market failure. Some phenomena such as *externalities, economies of scale,* and *uncertainty* tend to affect the efficiency of the market results. In these cases of market failure the price system still allocates resources, but the particular allocations to which it leads are not efficient. Phenomena such as *public goods* cause market failure because no markets for these goods even exist. Other phenomena such as *principal-agent problems* or *moral hazard* tend to arise when the goals of decisionmakers come into conflict with those of resource owners or with social norms.

A completely different type of market failure involves the question of equity. While markets may allocate resources and output efficiently, the allocation that results may be contrary to society's notions of equity or fairness. The market is a heartless taskmaster. Unlike our political philosophy of one person, one vote, the market operates under the dictum of one dollar, one vote. While under some circumstances it could be more efficient to allow the poor to live in despair, social conscience makes us remedy the situation even at the expense of economic efficiency.

The final section in this chapter explores the possibility of government intervention in the marketplace or other institutional changes that might improve the results of the market. Some of the problems caused by market failure, for example, can be remedied to various degrees by changing laws that hamper the formation or operation of certain markets, or by the direct substitution of government activity for markets that are too expensive or too difficult to establish any other way. But first we turn to a definition of economic efficiency that provides a benchmark against which we can measure the resource allocations dictated by unconstrained markets.

EFFICIENT MARKETS

Efficiency, for the economist, indicates the absence of costless improvements. The concept of efficiency is quite general and can be applied in any situation where there is a well-defined objective and some constraints on attaining that objective. An economic problem has been solved efficiently if it is impossible to find another solution that is closer to the objective. The economic problem of distribution, for example, is nothing other than the question of *for whom* to produce. If there were unlimited quantities of all goods and services, there would be no economic problem. We could simply give each individual all that he or she wanted. Unfortunately, in the real world resources and productive capacity are scarce. Therefore, the "best" distribution depends on our economic objective.

If we start by assuming that individuals are the best judges of their own likes and dislikes, it turns out that opportunities frequently arise to change some particular distribution of goods and services and make at least some one better off while making no one worse off. Unlike baseball, where there is always a winner and a loser at the end of every game, the game of economic exchange can easily end with only winners. Only after the available goods and services have been reallocated efficiently will any further exchange result in both winners and losers. But situations involving both winners and losers are beyond the scope of this chapter because they require choices based on conflicting values best left to political and social decision processes.

Characteristics of Efficient Allocations

Whenever one individual is willing to exchange commodities at a rate that differs from the rate at which some other individual is willing to exchange them, an opportunity exists for a mutually beneficial exchange. If, for example, A is willing to give up three oranges to get an apple, and B is willing to give up three apples to get an extra orange,

A and B can both be made better off through exchange. If A offers B one or two oranges for an apple, B should be delighted at the offer since B was willing to give up as many as three apples to get only a single orange. This example illustrates the condition for an efficient distribution of output as stated in Proposition 1.

Proposition 1: An efficient allocation of commodities between consumers requires that the rate at which one consumer is willing to exchange these commodities equals the rate at which any other consumer is willing to exchange them.

This observation about the distribution of goods and services to consumers applies equally to the questions of *what to produce* and *how to produce it.* These, for example, should be answered in such a way that it would be impossible to reshuffle the available resources between the different commodities or different producers of the same commodity and increase the output of any commodity or producer without reducing the output of some other commodity or producer.

Suppose that some producer could substitute three units of labor for one unit of capital (or vice versa) and keep its output rate constant. A second producer, perhaps because it produces a different commodity or uses a different production technique, can substitute labor for capital, unit for unit. Such a situation is not consistent with our notion of efficiency. We could, for example, shift one unit of capital from the second to the first producer—this step would free three units of labor. Only one of these units of labor would be required to sustain the original output rate of the second producer; the remaining two units of labor could be used somewhere else in the economy. Without having to give up anything, the output of something can be increased.

This example illustrates the condition for an efficient allocation of resources, as stated in Proposition 2.

Proposition 2: An efficient allocation of resources among producers requires that the rate at which inputs can be substituted (keeping the output rate constant) by one producer equals the rate at which they can be substituted by any other producer.

When all available resources are allocated efficiently to the various production processes, society is producing on its production possibilities frontier. The production possibilities frontier, based on the most efficient use of society's resources and technology, represents the constraints that ultimately bind consumer choices and limit the standard of living enjoyed by the society. Its slope represents the rate at which the economy is able to substitute commodities in production.

If the economy is operating efficiently, the rate at which it transforms one commodity into another must be exactly equal to the rate at which consumers are willing to exchange them. For example, let us assume that it is possible to increase wheat production by two bushels with the resources required to produce one bushel of corn. Exhibit 4-1 depicts this possibility as a movement from point A to point B along the production possibilities frontier. However, if consumers desire corn and wheat equally, then the economy has not selected an efficient point on its production possibilities frontier. If we reduced corn output by a bushel, for example, we could increase wheat output by two bushels. Since consumers would be willing to give up the bushel of corn as long as they got a bushel of wheat in return (a move from point A to point C), they would be elated at the prospect of receiving two extra bushels instead. Clearly they would be better off than before.

The condition for efficiency of the economy overall is stated in Proposition 3.

Proposition 3: An efficient allocation of resources requires that the rate at which consumers are willing to substitute commodities equals the rate at which it is technically possible to transform them.

If any of these conditions fails to hold, then the particular economic decisions that lay behind them were not efficient. They could not have been efficient because it should be possible to pick a different bundle of commodities, allocate resources differently between production processes, or distribute the commodities differently to consumers in some way that increases the welfare of at least one consumer and at the same time not reduce the welfare of any consumer. But these are the questions with which we started our analysis: *what* should the economy produce, *how* should the economy produce it, and *to whom* should the output be distributed?

We now know the answers to each of these questions. We should pick a production possibility where the rate at which we transform commodities—one into the other—is such that, if the output were distributed correctly, consumers would be willing to exchange those commodities at exactly the same rate.

The characteristics of an efficient economy have been described without any reference to institutional arrangements. We have not mentioned markets or prices or planners. We have not asked how such an efficient situation might come about. Our next task, therefore, is to investigate how a price system might lead to the same economic configuration as would a bureau of omniscient planners.

How Competitive Markets Achieve Efficient Results

Although there are probably a number of ways in which an efficient economy can be constructed, a system of perfectly competitive markets

Exhibit 4-1
Violation of Proposition 3

If the economy is currently producing at point A on the production possibilities frontier and if consumers are willing to sacrifice one unit of corn for the opportunity to consume an additional unit of wheat, resources are not efficiently allocated. Since point A is on the production possibilities frontier, production itself must be efficient (Proposition 2 is satisfied). It is even possible that all consumers are willing to exchange corn for wheat at the rate of one for one (Proposition 1 might be satisfied). But Proposition 3 is clearly not satisfied, since it is possible to shift the resources required for the production of one unit of corn into two units of wheat.

The implication is obvious. Consumers would consider themselves indifferent between consuming at point A or point C. Moving from A to C would require them to give up exactly one unit of corn for an additional unit of wheat. But that would free up enough resources to increase wheat output by two units. In fact, it would make possible the production of any combination of corn and wheat in the shaded area B-C-C'. Since all these have at least as much wheat and at least as much corn as point C, at least one individual could be made better off without any sacrifice for anyone else.

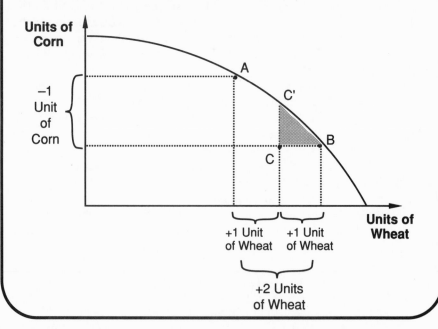

can accomplish the task easily. As Chapter 3 explained, the conditions of perfect competition create a price-taker's market, in which individual agents cannot affect market prices. We will assume that producers of commodities are interested in obtaining the greatest profits they can and that consumers are interested in translating their income into the greatest possible flow of utility.

According to the theory of rational choice, consumers increase their consumption of any particular commodity as long as the marginal utility per dollar exceeds the marginal benefits they expect to reap by spending their dollars elsewhere. When the consumer has done as well as possible, the ratio of prices of any two commodities represents the rate at which one is willing to substitute the commodities. Suppose that the price of apples is $1 per apple and the price of oranges is $2 per orange. Whatever the number of apples and oranges purchased, it must be true and the consumer is willing to trade two apples for an orange.

If, on the contrary, the consumer is really indifferent between apples and oranges, a different spending strategy would then lead to better results. The consumer could, for example, put an orange back on the shelf and take two apples instead. This strategy would cost the same amount of money, but would provide two extra apples instead of only a single orange. If we notice the ratio of prices

$$\frac{\$2 \text{ per orange}}{\$1 \text{ per apple}} = 2 \text{ apples per orange}$$

we observe that this is the rate at which the consumer is willing to exchange apples for oranges.

In competitive markets all consumers can obtain exactly the same terms of trade with producers. They all face the same market prices. But if the ratio of market prices is the rate at which consumers are willing to substitute commodities, then the fact that all consumers face the same set of market prices ensures that the efficiency condition in Proposition 1 holds.

A similar argument can be made to show that Proposition 2 holds if all producers try to maximize their profits and face the same set of market prices for their inputs. It is impossible for profits to be at a maximum if a firm does not operate at minimum cost. However, cost minimization requires that a firm hire factors of production as long as their marginal contribution to revenues exceeds their price. Again, unless it hires inputs in such a way that the ratio of their prices is equal to the rate at which they can be substituted in production, the firm cannot be minimizing its costs.

Suppose it is possible to substitute one unit of labor for two units of capital and keep the output level constant. Unless the price of labor is twice the price of capital, there is a way to increase profits. Suppose, for example, that labor costs $12 per hour and capital costs $8 per hour.

Since the output level (and therefore revenues) would stay the same if one unit of labor is substituted for two units of capital, and since this would reduce production costs by $4, the firm could not have been maximizing its profits.

In perfectly competitive markets the maximum attainable economic profit in the long run is zero. Therefore, if a firm does not maximize its profits, it will operate at a loss and will be driven out of business. The only firms that can survive are those that hire factors of production in such a way that cost reductions are impossible. But this condition can occur only when the rate at which inputs can be substituted equals the ratio of their prices. Again, notice that unless

$$\frac{\$8 \text{ per hour of capital}}{\$12 \text{ per hour of labor}} = \frac{2}{3} \text{ hour of labor per hour of capital}$$

is the rate at which labor can be substituted for capital, there will be some way of cutting costs and increasing profits. However, since all firms face the same market prices for their input, all firms must be able to substitute inputs at the same rate. This condition is what was required by Proposition 2.

We now can show how Proposition 3 will be satisfied if markets are competitive. Perfectly competitive firms will increase output until marginal cost has risen to the level of market price; but the marginal cost is the rate at which one commodity can be transformed into another. For example, if it is possible to increase the output of chairs by two chairs with the resources that are required to make a table, the marginal cost of a table is two chairs. Unless the market price of tables is twice that of chairs, there exists some unexploited profit opportunity in this economy.

Suppose, for example, that the market price of chairs is $20 per chair, and the market price of tables is $30. Since the resources required for a table can be turned into two chairs, any table manufacturer can reduce table output by one (a revenue loss of $30) and increase chair output by two (a revenue gain of $40) for a net increase in profits of $10. Firms that do not take advantage of such opportunities for profit will eventually be driven from the market. The result is that the rate at which consumers are willing to substitute commodities will equal the rate at which the production sector can transform them. Perfectly competitive markets lead to the most efficient allocation of resources.

A system of competitive prices guides the economy to allocations of resources and distributions of output that are consistent with overall efficiency of the economy. The self-interest of producers and consumers results in the exploitation of all potentially rewarding gains from trade.

In long-run equilibrium all three of the propositions that define efficiency will be satisfied. However, markets are never in long-run equilibrium.

REASONS FOR MARKET FAILURE

Markets work well when the prices they establish do their job properly. Their job is to coordinate and rationalize the choices of the many individual decisionmakers in a complex economy. To allocate resources efficiently, commodity prices should reflect consumers' marginal valuations of various goods and services. Resource prices should reflect the value of the best alternative use of the inputs. Whenever these marginal valuations and prices diverge, inefficiency exists and markets fail to send the proper signals. As a result, there will be unexploited opportunities for welfare gains.

Perhaps the divergence occurs because of market power. Price-searchers have market power because they can unilaterally increase the market price. Price-takers operating in perfectly competitive markets do not have any market power. Entry into the industry is so easy that whenever any firm tries to withhold part of its supply from the market to force up the price, new suppliers immediately take its place, and the strategy fails. Only effective barriers to entry or significant information problems enable firms to raise price above marginal cost, thus distorting the allocational signals of the market.

It is possible that the divergence occurs because the prices on which decisionmakers base their decisions, while they accurately capture the marginal valuations of the decisionmaker, fail to reflect proper marginal valuations of others. In such situations the existence of *externalities* causes markets to fail.

Other possible reasons for market failure relate to the fact that many important decisions have certain consequences in the future. While all of us have some concern for future generations, the extent to which we are willing to incur sizable costs for uncertain benefits is subject to speculation.

These and other "real world" complications might generate the wrong type of market signals. They are wrong in the sense that they lead to an inefficient allocation of resources and distribution of output.

Market outcomes can be undesirable in other ways as well. Markets may lead to technically efficient results, but these results can be inconsistent with social or political goals. That is, an efficient solution is not always an equitable solution. One reason is the difficulty of agreeing on a common definition of social goals or of equity. Another reason is that demand and supply are significantly affected by income. All prices, competitive or not, depend on the particular distribution of income. Even the income streams of resource owners, including labor, depend on the original distribution of income and historical accidents. If the wealth of the last generation had been distributed differently, the prices that exist today would be different. Incomes today would also be different.

Market Power

Market power arises when some firms are price-searchers rather than merely price-takers. The model of perfect competition assumes that no decisionmaker has any power over or influence upon market price. Everyone must take market prices as given and react to them. Since the cardinal rule of rational decisionmaking is to carry out any activity as long as the incremental benefit exceeds the incremental cost, producers increase output until marginal cost has risen to the level of market price. In perfectly competitive conditions marginal revenue equals price, which is the marginal value of the last unit of output to the consumer of that output. When a seller does have power over market price, a divergence between price and marginal revenue appears.

Market power means that someone has some control over price. Sellers can only control price if not all demand disappears when the seller raises his price. Some demand continues because consumers do not have enough perfect substitutes. Such a situation might arise if the number of suppliers is small and if there is some barrier to the entry of new suppliers. The implications of market power are primarily allocative. A seller interested in maximizing profits will still produce efficiently, that is, at lowest cost. Profit maximization, however, might not be as crucial for the survival of a noncompetitive firm.

It is probable, especially if the rest of the economy is competitive, that the raising of price above marginal cost leads to allocative inefficiency. If the monopolist were to increase output by one unit, that additional unit would be worth more to consumers than the current use of the requisite resources. In Exhibit 4-2, for example, everyone (including the monopolist) would gain if output were increased by one unit. It would add $p worth of satisfaction to some consumer and contribute $(p − mc) to the profits of the monopolist. From a social point of view, the producer with market power is producing the "wrong" level of output because everyone would be better off if output increased.

Collusion Sometimes market power enables market participants to protect their positions and exclude potential entrants. Strikes, for example, occur when workers bargaining with management seek to

Exhibit 4-2
Inefficiency of Price Greater than Marginal Cost

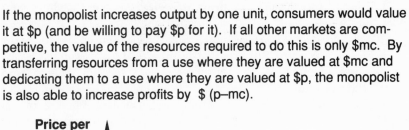

If the monopolist increases output by one unit, consumers would value it at $p (and be willing to pay $p for it). If all other markets are competitive, the value of the resources required to do this is only $mc. By transferring resources from a use where they are valued at $mc and dedicating them to a use where they are valued at $p, the monopolist is also able to increase profits by $ (p–mc).

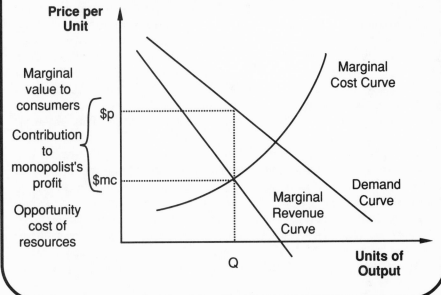

deprive management of labor services—not only from the strikers but also from those who would be willing to perform the same tasks as the strikers. Lockouts are an example of management refusing to let labor work. Workers are blacklisted, and they are not allowed to accept employment even at different companies.

In states with *union shops* or *closed shops,* union membership becomes essential for employment. A case can be made that unions, especially the craft unions, are able to raise wages by restricting entry into the field. In carpentry, masonry, or printing, the required skills are developed on the job, and the craft unions are able to restrict entry into apprenticeship program. In much the same way, the American Medical Association restricts entry into the medical profession by allowing only graduates of approved medical schools into the field each year and requiring a lengthy internship program.

Since *entry restrictions* impede new competition, they tend to keep the price high. "Buy American" programs, domestic content laws, and import quotas are all government-sanctioned ways of restricting competition and keeping prices high. Regulation and enforcement of these agreements and cartels frequently involve the government, since collusive agreement must be enforced to protect members from cheaters and encroachers.

Opportunities for collusion channel a significant volume of resources toward seeking and protecting such profits. These resources probably could be used more productively elsewhere in the economy. Because the cost of doing business in regulated industries has risen, exchange of the industry's output will still occur at a level where marginal cost equals marginal revenue. However, the marginal cost will include not only the direct resource costs but also the cost of protecting the industry from new competitors.

Collusion on the part of buyers is also possible. This action is usually called a *boycott*. The objectives are the same—to create market power through the removal of competition. If potential buyers can refuse to buy a product and prevent others from taking their place, they can reduce the demand for the product and reduce the resulting profits. But just as with sellers' boycotts, the problems are the same. Boycotts can induce short-run price reductions, but they cannot force permanent price reductions unless the industry operates under conditions of increasing cost. There is also an incentive to cheat. Someone who secretly buys after the boycott has driven the price down will benefit.

Economies of Plant Size Entrepreneurs might also be dissuaded from entering an industry where price exceeds average cost because there is essentially no room in the market for a new producer. Although existing suppliers might be earning positive economic profits, it might be that the additional sales that could be made at marginal cost prices are not sufficient to sustain a plant large enough to take advantage of available economies of scale. In such a situation no prospective entrant would have any hope that revenues would cover total cost. If a firm cannot cover its total cost of production, it certainly would not choose to enter such an industry.

This situation could arise when production exhibits decreasing average costs throughout the relevant range of demand. If unit production costs decline throughout the output levels for which demand exists (as in Panel A of Exhibit 4-3), the industry will eventually become a monopoly. This is the case of natural monopoly.

If the output level at which all economies of scale are exhausted is relatively large compared to the market quantity demanded at that price (as in Panel B of Exhibit 4-3), the industry is naturally oligopolistic. In either case the market will not be characterized by a large number of producers. And when there are few suppliers of a commodity, the number of perfect substitutes for the output of any particular producer is correspondingly small. As the available substitutes are less perfect, the consumer generally will be less inclined to make substitutions in the face of price increases. This absence of good substitutes gives monopolists and oligopolists their market power.

In addition, if there are significant investments in specialized capital required in this industry, there will not be a large number of potential competitors eagerly waiting to take advantage of any positive profits earned by oligopolists or monopolists. In a situation where entry or the threat of entry does not force the market price down to the level of marginal cost, because at that level maximum profits are negative, the market fails to establish prices that lead to an efficient allocation of resources. This situation is commonly called a natural barrier to entry.

The fact that a market has few producers does not, however, prove that such a natural barrier to entry exists. Perhaps the barriers are unnatural—decreed by the government, as in the case of television broadcast stations. If the barrier is truly natural and if the efficiency loss caused by nonmarginal cost pricing is so serious that its elimination could potentially offset the certain cost of altering the market result, the situation requires market intervention.

There are essentially two options. We can artificially constrain the size of each firm. That would create a market with many small firms. But since none of these firms would be able to take advantage of the economies of large-scale production, this solution would be a waste of resources and therefore inefficient. A second option would be government regulation of price, as in the case of public utilities. While there can be a significant cost associated with this kind of regulation, it may well improve the result of no regulation.

Transportation, Transaction, and Information Costs It might seem that not much good comes from the existence of significant economies of scale. However, it is their very existence that makes our economy so productive. It is the advantage of specialization that allows us to stretch our resources. If there were no advantage in large-scale production, there would be no need for business firms. We could all be self-sufficient producer-consumer units.

Nevertheless, the advantages of specialization are available only at a cost. As soon as individuals are no longer self-sufficient, they must create some sort of mechanism for facilitating exchange. Since

Exhibit 4-3
Economies of Plant Size

Panel A

NATURAL MONOPOLY—only one optimally sized
plant is required to service the market.

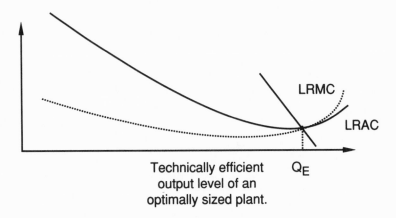

Technically efficient
output level of an
optimally sized plant. Q_E

Panel B

NATURAL OLIGOPOLY—only a small number of optimally
sized plants are required to service the market.

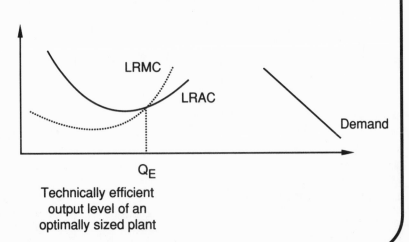

Q_E
Technically efficient
output level of an
optimally sized plant

production and consumption no longer take place at the same location or at the same time, distances of space and time must somehow be bridged.

As Adam Smith suggested, competition is limited by the extent of the market. If economies of scale are exhausted at output levels that are small relative to the quantity demanded in the market, the market can support a large number of sellers and is more likely to be competitive. The existence of significant economies of large-scale production might result in a minimum efficient level of operation that is large relative to the quantity demanded in the market. This situation might lead to a reduction in the number of competitors, giving some control of price to the remaining supplier or suppliers.

Anything that increases the full cost of commodities also limits the extent of the market and increases the potential market power of suppliers. When the cost of simply making a transaction becomes significant, the value of markets as efficient allocators is impeded. Conversely, anything that reduces transactions costs increases the extent of the market and tends to undermine whatever market power suppliers might have.

Improved transportation and communication systems reduce the friction of distance that adds to transactions costs. As these systems develop, market areas widen and support larger numbers of competitors. Such a reduction of economic distance makes it less costly to transport commodities, gain access to services, or gather information about market opportunities and relative terms of exchange in distant locales. The European Economic Community, for example, widens domestic markets for European producers by reducing the obstacles imposed by national boundaries.

The competitive model of choice assumes that costs and benefits, which guide consumer and producer actions, are known with certainty. It also assumes that the quality of information is the same (perfect) for both parties to a transaction. In real life, of course, few things are certain. And rarely do buyers and sellers have the same quality of information about the terms of trade. Yet, these real-life conditions do less damage to the conclusions we have reached than might be expected.

Some decisions often are made again and again, such as where to eat lunch each day. The choices might include fast food in the restaurant on the corner, a sandwich in the office, or haute cuisine at a restaurant that just opened across town.

We might know little about the new restaurant. We could drive over, walk in, and look at the menu (expending scarce resources in search of information), or we could simply ask friends about the food and prices. But we cannot really know what the food will taste like until we try some. When we do, there is the possibility that we will be disappointed. If greatly disappointed, we can send the food back and try again, refuse to pay, or sue the restaurant. However, we will probably just chalk it up to experience and not eat there again.

For some decisions we can simply try an option and evaluate the results. If the decision must be made with some regularity, and if the consequences of mistakes, while certainly regrettable, are not particularly injurious or expensive, this might not be a bad way to proceed. We can learn from mistakes and let experience guide future decisions. It might be appropriate in most circumstances to consider these search costs as a normal part of the transaction cost.

In other instances this approach does not work nearly as well. When we are critically ill and need medical attention, the assurance that we could sue for malpractice if the care is not appropriate provides little comfort. When choices are irreversible or not frequently made, mistakes can be extremely costly. We cannot merely depend on market forces to drive out incompetent surgeons in the same way that competitive market forces drives out incompetent restaurateurs. There are some circumstances for which financial compensation can never be sufficient. In such situations markets do not send the proper signals. Without some way to reduce the consumer's uncertainty—perhaps through some system of regulation—too many of the potential benefits from specialization and exchange will be consumed as a hedge against uncertain outcomes, and the level of economic activity will be stunted.

While some transactions involve direct exchanges of one good for another, most transactions involve monetary payments. Selling something for money occurs in the expectation that the money can later be exchanged for more useful goods. The value of money comes from its expected future use. Once we lose faith in the exchangeability of money, that money loses some of its value. To the extent that money becomes a less acceptable means of exchange, some of the efficiency of market exchanges will be lost. The cost of exchange itself will rise, and the benefit derived from exchange will be reduced. Anything that drives a wedge between the amount paid by the buyer and the amount received by the seller reduces the potential gains from specialization and exchange.

Externalities

Rational decisionmakers continue an activity as long as the marginal benefits of the activity exceed the marginal costs of the activity. It is therefore critically important that producers and consumers accurately perceive the benefits and costs associated with their activities.

The competitive market model depends on the assumption that consumers and producers receive all the benefits that result from their decisions and incur all the costs those decisions entail. When some of these benefits or costs spill over onto other individuals who are not party to the decision, we say that there are *externalities.* Externalities may be good or bad. If the decisionmakers do not derive all the benefits resulting from their decisions, they will not carry out the activity at a sufficiently high rate. Similarly, if they do not incur all the costs associated with the activity, they will be tempted to exceed the efficient rate. Because of the externality, their private costs are less than the actual costs of the activity.

An extreme example of externalities is when none of the benefits from a production decision can be captured through the marketplace. Certain kinds of goods are peculiar in that once they are provided, no one can be excluded from their consumption. Such goods are called *public goods* and markets in which they are traded do not exist. Rational consumers generally have no incentive to record their preferences for these goods. They prefer to let others pay for their provision and then to take a "free ride."

Externalities in Production and Consumption In some instances, buyers and sellers may not take into consideration all the costs and benefits associated with a particular transaction. It may happen that as a result of the transaction some costs or some benefits may spill over and affect third parties. Such spillover effects may be either good or bad from the point of view of the unintended recipient. They create or destroy value external to the immediate transaction.

In general, when beneficial externalities occur, someone receives a benefit from a transaction but does not share in the cost. Not all the benefit of the transaction accrues to the decisionmaker. If a firm intends to expand until its marginal cost equals its marginal benefit but does not receive all of the marginal benefit experienced by society, the firm is induced to operate at a privately optimal but socially suboptimal level. Panel A in Exhibit 4-4 shows this situation. Because the firm does not derive all the benefit from its actions, it produces only at the Q_1 level. If, however, the firm could receive the full benefit, it would produce at the Q_2 level.

Panel B of Exhibit 4-4 shows a similar misallocation because of an externality in costs. If the firm does not have to bear the full cost or consequence of its decisions, it will produce at a level greater than the socially optimal rate. Since the firm can pass on part of the cost with impunity, there is nothing to prevent it from exceeding Q_1, the point where social marginal cost equals private marginal benefit. It will produce at the Q_2 level instead because it can avoid some of the cost.

Exhibit 4-4
Effects of Externalities.

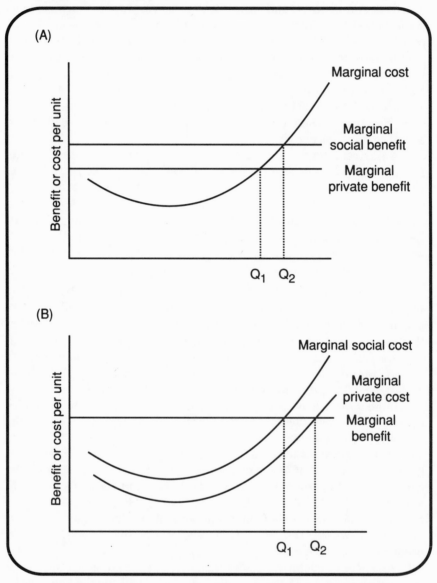

Not all externalities are harmful. Consumption of education, for example, might make the consumer more aware and a better citizen and therefore benefit society as a whole. The individuals who bear the cost of education, however, gain only a part of the total benefits. Unless costs are somehow reduced, through subsidies to education, for example, individuals will not be encouraged to consume the optimal amount of education.

Similarly, neighbors benefit when homeowners keep their lawns neat and well-trimmed and their houses painted. Individual activity improves the property value in the neighborhood. Yet individuals cannot capture any of this additional benefit. Chances are, therefore, that they underestimate the true marginal social benefit of their industry and will stop improving their property before it has reached its optimal level of quality.

Industrial Accidents and Occupational Disease Whenever decisionmakers either do not incur the full social cost or receive the full social benefit of their decisions, they are likely to make a privately efficient, but socially inefficient, choice. One way in which individuals can avoid the full social cost of their actions is to rely on social insurance. If social insurance is funded through assessments based on any criteria other than the prospect of losses engendered by the insured, then the decisionmaker is able to pass part of the cost of his decision on to the rest of the payers into the insurance fund.

For example, consider production processes that have high rates of industrial accidents or occupational disease. One would expect that in a world of perfect knowledge, workers in such industries would be aware of the risks they were taking and would accept employment only if the wages were sufficient to cover the expected hazards to their health. The risk would presumably be insurable at some price, and that price would have to be part of the wage premium paid. If, however, the employee is also covered by social insurance funded by taxes, part of the expected cost is passed on to society.

The employer also is aware that certain compensation programs for which the employees are eligible are funded in ways that are not related to the loss experience of that particular factory. The employer will be tempted, since the firm will not pay for the full loss or for the actuarily fair insurance cost, to be less than optimally careful. The firm will have to incur private costs in terms of outlays on equipment or reduced employee productivity because of safer work rules. However, it will not receive the full benefit in terms of reduced insurance payments or expected damage payment. Therefore it will not carry out safety improvement programs to their efficient level.

Limited liability also puts a cap on the award that the corporation is expected to pay. Bankruptcy is a solution for makers of asbestos, fertilizer, and other chemicals, and for toxic waste handlers.

The workers' compensation insurance system provides a mechanism to include the costs of industrial accidents in the private costs of production, thus reducing a potential externality. In theory, at least, a more efficient allocation of resources results because decisionmakers must incorporate the costs of workers' compensation in their calculations. In countries where taxpayers bear the costs of industrial accidents, firms in hazardous industries are more likely to overproduce.

Pollution   Pollution is another example of the failure to consider the relevant costs associated with a particular production decision. Production requires the use of many inputs, most of which must be bought and paid for in the market. The reason that they must be paid for is that they belong to someone, and unless compensated, their owners normally would be unwilling to part with them. As long as all markets are competitive, the prices at which trades occur will reflect fully the marginal valuation of the resources in their best alternative use. Profit maximizing producers allocate resources only to those employments where the benefit is at least as large as the cost.

Unfortunately, there are some resources that do not belong to any particular individual. Clean air and water obviously do have value to the members of society. Yet since no one has title to these resources, there cannot be any legitimate sellers, market, or price. As a result, consumers of these resources will treat them as though they were free.

When producers can use resources without having to pay for them, however, they tend to use too much of them. This tendency is at the heart of many pollution problems. As long as the environment has value in excess of the price that users have to pay for its destruction, the market system fails to deal efficiently with the issue of environmental quality.

Before we look at different kinds of pollution, we need to address a common misconception about it. Pollution is not intrinsic to any particular activity. Rather, it results when the total complex of production processes affects the environment to such a degree that its quality begins to deteriorate perceptibly. We interpret pollution as an uncompensated reduction in use-value of the environment.

Thus pollution is not the discharge of smoke into the atmosphere, nor the dumping of waste into rivers, streams, or landfills. Pollution results from the excess of such activity. This excess is what creates the externality. Emitters of smoke into the atmosphere, for example, are not necessarily polluting. Neither are most dumpers of waste. Pollution occurs only when too many emitters and dumpers are carrying out their activity in a localized area.

The environment has a certain capacity to absorb the things that humans inflict upon it. Properly oxygenated water (and the life it supports) can decompose a particular volume of garbage per period of time. The atmosphere can disperse particular volumes of chemicals and solids to imperceptible levels. A highway can accommodate a certain volume of traffic so that normally no driver is affected by another. If any of these activities occurs at sufficiently high levels, however, the capacity of the system to absorb such usage is approached. Eventually the quality of the system begins to decrease. This is when pollution occurs—when an additional user begins to strain the ability of the system to support existing use without a reduction in quality.

Air and water are examples of resources for which markets have not developed to any great extent. Air is used by almost every production process imaginable. Yet very little air is bought and sold in markets. Although compressed air is sold to scuba divers, "just plain air" seems to be available for the taking. Since it has no price, users of air treat it as though it were not a scarce resource.

In many localities, especially heavily industrialized ones, clean air is scarce. The polluted air that replaces it imposes significant costs on others. It fouls the lungs, irritates the eyes, and increases mortality and morbidity rates. Acids in polluted air can destroy or severely damage buildings, cars, and corn fields. Suspended solids can dirty one's house or clothes. Since real costs are imposed on society by the existence of pollution, they cannot be ignored.

Reasonable people might be willing to incur additional costs for the more frequent dry cleaning of their wardrobes necessitated by the soot emitted by the factory across the street, but they generally will insist on compensation. To the extent that polluters can force others to incur such costs without compensation, an externality exists and a market distortion results.

A similar situation arises with water. Although some of us buy water in bottles, most of the time water is assumed to be freely available, at least in the East when there is not a drought. In the West water is perceived to be more scarce and is subject to far greater control. During periods of drought, even in the East, water is rationed and certain uses are precluded.

A variety of industries use prodigious amounts of water from rivers or lakes for cooling or cleaning. They then dump the heated or dirtied water back into the river or lake. As a result, any downstream user must spend money to restore the water to its former state before it can be used again. The increased temperature of the water used for cooling reduces its ability to hold dissolved oxygen. This reduces the ability of the water to support aquatic life and to degrade other pollutants.

We are only now becoming aware of the costs imposed on us by the chemical wastes dumped in the last several decades. Since these costs were essentially avoided by those who produced the wastes, such wastes have been produced in too great an abundance. Had the processes that generated the waste been charged for proper disposal, the cost of their output would have been larger. This would have led to a reduced output level (of the primary commodity as well as of the waste by-products) or a shift to technologies that generated less harmful (and therefore cheaper to dispose of) waste.

Public Goods   We can think of the production of pollution as the provision of *public bads*. Pollution forces us to consume lower levels of environmental quality without compensation from those who benefit from the destruction of that environment. Public and social goods are the same sort of thing, but in reverse. They are the goods and services that increase the quality of our environment without our having to pay those who provide them.

Public goods have characteristics that make it impossible to exclude anyone from consuming them once they have been provided. Furthermore, no one's consumption of public goods is reduced by the level at which others consume them. They represent an extreme case of externalities. Typical examples are national defense and flood control. Once an adequate level of national defense is provided, it becomes impossible to exclude individuals from the protection that exists. We cannot charge admission to defended areas.

The inability to exclude consumers effectively from the consumption of goods will lead to the failure of markets to make them available. A rational individual, for example, might consider producing some particular good or service generally deemed to be desirable, but also recognize that it would be impossible to charge a fee to those making use of the service, since it is impossible to exclude anyone. If someone else were to provide the service, then it would be impossible for that individual to exclude anyone. Therefore, the rational thing to do is to wait for someone else to provide the service. Of course, if everyone is rational, no one will provide the service that everyone deems to be desirable.

Nonexcludability causes market failure because a good that is of value to consumers, but for which they have no incentive to pay, will not be produced in a private enterprise system. Somehow people must be persuaded to pay for the service. A strong sense of community spirit or loyalty is frequently sufficient motivation for paying one's "fair share" to some particular project. Other situations, however, may require taxes or assessments.

Goods such as roads and bridges are not quite public goods, but have similar effects. It is possible to exclude individual users from sidewalks, city streets, and highways if they refuse to pay a required toll. However, the technology of toll assessment and collection is such that it can impose an unacceptable resource cost if usage levels are precisely measured and billed. It is therefore generally not regarded as desirable for these services to be provided by the market.

There is an additional consideration. If the facility is not congested, then the social marginal cost of an additional user is probably near zero. This suggests that a zero price should be charged if the facility is to be utilized at an efficient level—even if it is feasible to collect a fee. But if the efficient price is zero, the facility will generate no revenue. No entrepreneur would consider constructing it. Only an entrepreneur who could restrict access and charge a price sufficient to meet the costs would construct it. This, however, would lead to a social underutilization of the facility. It would waste resources. For this reason, public and social goods are usually provided by the government and funded through a combination of use and general taxes.

At this point, it might be worthwhile to reiterate that the market failure we are considering arises primarily from the nonexcludability of the public good. Such nonexcludability, however, is a property of the way the commodity is consumed, not of how it is produced. There is no reason to believe that the government necessarily has any particular advantage over the private enterprise system in the production of public goods. The fact that a competitive price system cannot efficiently allocate resources to a good or service for which prices cannot or should not be charged does not imply that the competitive price system could not effectively allocate resources to its production once the appropriate output level has been picked by some nonmarket mechanism.

In other words, the market is defeated because maximum profits are negative when output levels are positive and revenues are zero. As long as social benefits are positive, the market system provides the wrong answer to the question, *what to produce.* But if the correct answer could be decided in some other way, the price system still could be relied upon to provide the correct answer to the question, *how to produce.* While the government may need to extract the resource costs from consumers in some nonmarket fashion, this does not mean that the government should also coordinate production.

Uncertainty and Time Horizon

We have already discussed how information asymmetries might impede the operation of markets at efficient levels. When buyers and sellers do not have access to the same quality of information, efficiency losses result. However, what if the information asymmetry is not between parties to a particular transaction, but between different points in time? We may not know what the closing price of pork bellies was on the commodities exchange last week. Therefore, our purchasing decisions in the bacon market are to some extent uninformed.

Generating this type of information, however, is intrinsically different from the problem of ascertaining the closing price of pork bellies two months from now. Information about the past can be collected; information about the future is more speculative.

We have argued that the proper level at which any economic activity ought to be carried out (at least if the objective is efficiency) is where marginal costs rise to the level of marginal benefits. The proper notion of cost is opportunity cost, the value of the best forgone alternative. The only costs that should affect any decision are the values of the precluded option, the alternatives that will cease to exist. However, this decision rule leads to a rather ticklish problem. Once a decision is made and the alternative is in fact forgone, how can we measure the exact value of these alternatives? If we do not choose these options, we can never experience them. Since all costs are values of things not done, they can only be estimated. But, no matter how reasonable the estimate or the forecast, we will never know for sure.

Some things usually can be estimated more closely than others. For example, we might know with reasonable certainty that going to the movies tonight will cost $4.00 for the ticket, $1.00 in transportation, $5.00 for refreshments, and three hours of travel and movie watching time. If we have read rave reviews or heard favorable reports from friends, we may decide that the movie is worth it. But what if we had to incur the costs right now and could go to see the movie tomorrow, next week, or ten years from now? Something would surely be different in these cases. Whenever the costs and the benefits associated with any activity are separated in time, there is something else at work. Most people put some sort of premium on how soon benefits can be enjoyed, but they are almost always eager to put costs farther into the future.

Humans have a tendency to discount the future. The value or cost of an activity tends to decrease the farther into the future it is likely to be realized. If the costs (consequences) of an action are very far into the future, it often takes only a small immediate benefit to justify the action. For one thing, the farther into the future the costs or benefits of an action arise, the more uncertain their realization becomes. The world could be different. Circumstances could change. The more difficult it becomes to estimate the expected costs and benefits, the more we tend to discount them.

In many instances the future consequences of today's actions are impossible to foresee. But in some cases we could form some reasonable expectations if we dedicated some resources to the search. Perhaps the lasting and profound impacts on the food chain were not foreseen when DDT was first introduced. Perhaps they could not have been. However, some of the possible consequences of prolonged exposure to asbestos dust, coal dust, cigarette smoke, and PCBs were suspected for some time, but some of the initial research findings were not publicized as widely or as early as might have been desirable.

It is certainly not a case of market failure if actions have long-range consequences that could not possibly have been foreseen. But if diligence is not exercised in forming and publicizing expectations of reasonable consequences because of potential damage to specific interests, a case of market failure occurs.

Risk and Uncertainty While the future is unknowable, our expectations are not completely unfounded. Expectations about the near or intermediate future tend (although not universally) to be held more strongly than those about the more distant future. Expectations about events that are within the realm of ordinary experience have more force than those about events that can be only vaguely anticipated.

Most individuals are averse to risk. When the stakes are relatively small, many still gamble. But as the stakes grow larger, most require a premium for accepting risk or uncertainty. The result is another wedge between the costs and benefits from production and exchange. Any risk or uncertainty attached to the realization of the expected benefits of a transaction lowers its net value (benefits minus costs). As a result, the volume of such transactions will be reduced.

Anything that reduces the risk or uncertainty associated with a contemplated activity increases the net value of that activity. This is one of the advantages of insurance. Insurance can convert individual uncertainty into collective risk. And while uncertainty is not generally insurable, risk is. With insurance, individual uncertainty can be essentially eliminated through the payment of a fixed premium. Because some of the subjective elements in the assessment of uncertainty are eliminated through insurance, the efficiency of markets is increased.

Moral Hazard and Adverse Selection While insurance provides a mechanism for the sharing of risk among similarly situated decisionmakers, the mechanism is subject to certain problems. Insurance is efficient because it allows the pooling of risk, and it makes the future more certain for insured individuals.

It is possible, however, that insured individuals, simply because they are insured, will exercise less diligence and thereby increase the total risk to be shared. Someone insured against theft, for example, might be less inclined to have doors locked and to take other reasonable precautions to guard property. To the extent that mere existence of insurance leads to an increase in the amount of risk to be shared, *moral hazard* is said to exist. It is inefficient because it creates an incentive to increase the costs that are shared.

The problem of *adverse selection* resembles the problem of moral hazard in that it also leads to inefficiency. In insurance situations, adverse selection tends to increase the size of the risk simply because of the existence of insurance. While moral hazard is an issue as long as the insurer cannot identify the individuals who take advantage of the system by failing to exercise due diligence or by purposely engaging in riskier activity, adverse selection occurs when the risk shared by the pool is increased because the insurer cannot identify or sufficiently discriminate between groups with different risk characteristics. Adverse selection occurs if an individual insured has more information about the degree of risk than does the underwriter. People have more desire to buy life insurance, for example, if they know they are in poor health. Individuals who perceive the insurance premiums for their class to be a bargain, and are therefore likely to buy it, are also likely to be the ones who are the worst risks.

There will always be some variability of risk within any particular risk group. Both moral hazard and adverse selection stem from information asymmetry and drive up the premiums that must be charged for any particular coverage. Since this increased cost is essentially due to the increased size of the risk pool, it represents a misallocation of resources.

Principal-Agent Problems

Throughout our analysis we have focused on the motivation of the decisionmaker. We have maintained that an activity will continue as long as the perceived benefit exceeds the perceived cost from the point of view of the decisionmaker. Frequently, however, individuals form a group—a family, a business firm, or a government—that we speak of as the decisionmaking unit. But it is often too cumbersome for groups to make decisions. Usually individuals make decisions, and the individual decisions are then ratified somehow, perhaps through voting, persuasion, or intimidation.

If the person who owns the resources (the principal) delegates the decisionmaking power to a manager (the agent), the owner must take care to present the manager with a proper set of incentives. The manager-nonowner also is a rational optimizing agent. If left to their own devices, they make themselves as well off as possible. They engage in activities as long as the expected benefit (to them) exceeds the expected cost (to them).

If the owners of the resources are not careful, the managers may underestimate the cost of resources for which they have no personal use or which cannot be overtly converted to personal use. The boss would object if the manager cleared out the corporate bank account in order to buy a new sailboat or to vacation on the Riviera. But the manager might try to persuade the owner that the company needs a yacht on which to entertain clients or that the best place for the next department meeting is in St. Tropez.

Profits and losses provide the signals that move the economic system back toward a new, efficient allocation after a change in tastes or preferences, technology, or resource availability. For measured profits and losses to be effective in this regard, these profits and losses must be the result of profit maximizing activity. Sometimes, especially when markets are not very competitive, the urgency of profit maximization diminishes, and other objectives predominate.

In perfectly competitive markets in long-run equilibrium, maximum profits are zero; therefore, anyone who does not earn the largest possible profit must be losing money and will eventually be driven out of business. But in the short run, positive profits are the result of changing market conditions and the size of the profit or loss might well determine the speed with which output expansion or contraction adjustments occur.

If anyone in the firm has a private incentive that is inconsistent with profit maximization for the firm, a principal-agent problem is said to exist. The agents (salespeople, buyers, assembly line workers, or chief operating officers) have incentives that often deviate from the maximization of the firm's profit. Salespeople profit from extra-long lunches with friends rather than clients. Buyers who receive Christmas presents or tickets to football games from their suppliers are adding a cost to the items they buy. Office workers who meter their private mail on the office mail meter, make personal copies on the office copier, or call their out-of-town friends from the office phone shift personal living expenses onto the cost of their employer's product. These activities add to the benefits received by workers and may well be considered part of their pay. But to the extent that they could have been provided at lower resource cost, they represent an economic inefficiency. After all, consumers will never be made worse off if they receive cash instead of the same dollar's worth of specific commodities.

Distribution of Income and Equity

Because scarcity is inescapable, although perhaps manageable, some sort of rationing must occur. The price system, when markets are perfectly competitive, leads to an efficient allocation of resources. Unfortunately, efficiency is not the same thing as social desirability. The description of the competitive model includes a critical qualifying phrase, dependent upon the income distribution. This is the focal point in the whole discussion. For any given income distribution, a system of

Exhibit 4-5
Perfectly Equal Distribution of Income

Number of House-holds	Percent of House-holds	Cumulative Percentage of House-holds	Income of Each House-hold	Percent of Income Received by Each House-hold	Cumulative Percentage of Income
1	20%	20%	$10,000	20%	20%
2	20%	40%	10,000	20%	40%
3	20%	60%	10,000	20%	60%
4	20%	80%	10,000	20%	80%
5	20%	100%	10,000	20%	100%
	100%		$50,000	100%	

competitive prices will lead to an efficient allocation of resources and distribution of commodities. Any particular allocation of resources and distribution of output can be achieved as the result of the workings of competitive markets if we start with an appropriate distribution of income.

How income is distributed in a society is an important economic question with political, social, and ethical implications. *Size distribution of income* refers to the pattern of income shares received by different groups of households. Typically we divide the total number of households into ten or five groups, each representing 10 percent or 20 percent of the total households. If we divide households into five groups, for example, then we are interested in the percentage of total income received by each of the five quintiles of total households. The graph expressing the resulting pattern of income distribution is called a *Lorenz Curve.*

Suppose we have a society of five households, each receiving 20 percent of the total income in the society, as shown in Exhibit 4-5. A Lorenz Curve is constructed by plotting on a graph the cumulative percentage of total income (Column 6) against the cumulative percentage of households (Column 3). This information will produce a Lorenz Curve, which is a straight line with a 45-degree angle as shown in Exhibit 4-6. This diagonal line is designated as the *line of perfect equality* of income distribution since the total income is equally distributed among the five households.

However, the pattern of income distribution in real life always shows some degree of inequality. Suppose the pattern we have in a society is represented by the table in Exhibit 4-7. The Lorenz Curve for

Exhibit 4-6
Illustration of a Lorenz Curve

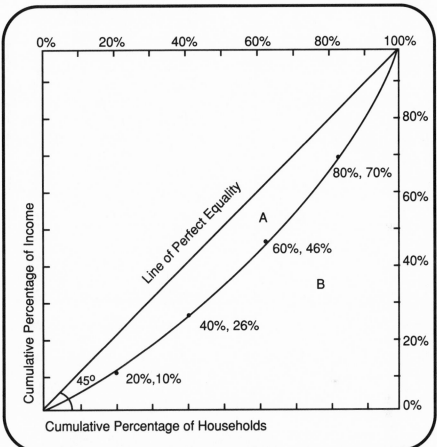

this income distribution will be the second in Exhibit 4-6, below the straight diagonal line. This new line is obtained, as before, by plotting the figures in Column 6 against those in Column 3. The percentages in Column 6 are shown by dots which, when connected by lines between successive pairs of dots, produce a new line. The new line is the Lorenz Curve for the unequal pattern of income distribution.

The proportion of the total triangular area under the line of perfect equality that lies between the Lorenz Curve and the diagonal line indicates the degree of income inequality. In Exhibit 4-6 it is the ratio of Area A to Area A + B. The closer the Lorenz Curve is to the line of perfect equality, the more equal is income distribution.

Different individuals naturally have different perceptions of the equity of a particular pattern of income distribution. Economic science

Exhibit 4-7

An Example of Unequal Distribution of Income

(1) House- holds	(2) Percent of House- holds	(3) Cumulative Percentage of House- holds	(4) Total Income of Each House- hold	(5) Percent of Income Received by Each House- hold	(6) Cumulative Percentage of Income
1	20%	20%	$5,000	10%	10%
2	20%	40%	8,000	16%	26%
3	20%	60%	10,000	20%	46%
4	20%	80%	12,000	24%	70%
5	20%	100%	15,000	30%	100%
	100%		$50,000	100%	

alone cannot evaluate the relative desirability of alternative economic arrangements as long as they are all efficient. Equity is largely a question of moral judgment.

Whatever the forces of markets dictate, while it might be efficient, it need not be socially desirable. Questions of equity are difficult. While most people would probably find fault with an economic system in which the great bulk of the wealth and consumption power accrued to a single individual, or even a handful, few would be prepared to define which of the many feasible alternative distributions of income is, in fact, the best. Even if we all thought we knew which was the best income distribution, it is extremely unlikely that our opinions would agree. It is doubtful that any proposed optimal distribution of income would receive unanimous approval.

We might be tempted to consider a completely equal distribution as the fairest. As long as people's tastes and preferences are not uniform, however, it will, in general, not be optimal to insist on an equal distribution of income. Expectation of income or lack of income is precisely what motivates most individuals to convert some of their available time from leisure time to labor hours. While there may be individuals who so dearly love their jobs that they would continue them no matter what, the majority of individuals respond to income signals. If everyone had a guaranteed equal income, many individuals would no longer have an incentive to contribute to employments where they would add the most. People would work the jobs they enjoyed the most, rather than those in which they were the most productive. The price system would lose its power to allocate resources to their most productive uses, and allocative inefficiency would result. The total output of the economy would decline.

While we may decry the existing distribution of income, we must be careful that our reform does not destroy those things the market system can do well. Social goals may very well supersede efficiency goals, but we ought to be aware of the costs at which we obtain greater equity. The danger is that we forget that scarcity always will force some rationing—some discrimination and selectivity. It is neither the price system nor capitalism that forces us to make unpleasant choices. It is the scarcity of resources in the face of unlimited human wants and desires that forces the choices. Any reform of the income distribution should carefully weigh the consequences for the overall size of the economic pie. Even the oppressed might prefer to have a small share of a large pie rather than a more equal share of a much smaller pie.

REMEDIES FOR MARKET FAILURE

In theory, there are a variety of ways in which economic relations can be arranged. Perhaps tradition dictates certain uses for resources. Perhaps some powerful force or government makes the allocation decisions and has the power to make sure they are followed. Perhaps markets develop that make the allocation decisions. If these markets are competitive, then the allocations they force will be efficient. When markets are not competitive or if they do not exist, it may be appropriate for government to step in and alter the results.

There are several options for government in its attempt to correct the allocations that result when markets have failed to yield efficient or equitable results. The government might try to restructure the rules under which markets are allowed to operate. The problem of externalities arises because some consequences of economic decisions escape detection in existing markets. If the government could somehow broaden the "field of vision" of the market, fewer consequences would escape detection and would be more likely to be included in the cost-benefit calculations of decisionmakers. If more of the essential conditions for perfect competition could be created, or at least simulated, by government action, the restructured markets could be relied on to improve efficiency.

When the sources of market failure are so fundamental, or when the costs of their correction are so great as to make the restructuring approach impossible or economically inefficient, a more direct attempt to regulate activity might be tried by the government. While this approach has been adopted frequently, we are now becoming more aware of its potential problems. The study of regulatory bureaucracies and the resource costs they directly or indirectly impose on society has become the focus of debate. Regulation is itself an economic activity subject to precisely the same potential failings as are the production and marketing of any other commodity.

Redefining Old Markets and Simulating Better Markets

If the market system is to do its job, all relevant information about relative scarcities must be incorporated in market prices. This essentially requires that the full effect of every decision must be captured by the appropriate markets. Notice that the requirement has two parts. All effects must be captured, and they must be captured by the appropriate market.

Extending Property Rights One way to improve the results of market allocations is to assign ownership of resources to private individuals. Resources have varying degrees of private ownership potential. Some enclosed bodies of water and the air in some enclosed spaces can be privately owned. One can, for example, legally restrict smoking within a building.

Free-flowing water and unenclosed air, however, generally have no identifiable owners. They tend to be treated as communal resources. It is this communality of ownership that tends to lead to market failure. The economic meaning of conservation is the decision to allocate a resource to the activity that generates the largest benefit. But in the case of communal resources, this tends to mean that resources are devoted to any use that generates a quick return even if returns to future uses are demonstrably greater.

Owners of private property are willing to forego immediate use of their resources as long as their future use has a greater present value. But no one has an ownership claim to communal resources. Someone who sees an opportunity for relatively low-value, current exploitation would be foolish not to seize it. If not exploited today, the resource will certainly be gone when the time for a more productive use arrives because someone else will have used it. There is no sure way to conserve a resource without owning it and legally keeping others from exploiting it.

To the extent that there are no technological impediments, it is the government that decides what sorts of resources may or may not be privately owned and the extent to which those ownership rights will be legally transferable. If we are interested in the most economically efficient use of our resources, an increase in the extent of private property will reduce the current failure of some markets. Again, however, we must be careful to remember that the current distribution of income helps to determine the current system of prices and, therefore, social valuations. The economically appropriate degree of environmental conservation is not an absolute; it is a function of the income distribution.

As incomes rise, for example, the "acceptable" level of environmental pollution tends to decrease. When incomes or standards of living are relatively low, toleration of reductions in environmental quality tend to be greater. A clean environment means an unused environment (or an environment used at higher cost) and can be more easily afforded by those who already enjoy a relatively high standard of living.

Internalizing Costs and Benefits Externalities exist when not all costs and benefits associated with a particular decision accrue to the decisionmakers. A divergence between private and social welfare is created. Producers, for example, will pay only those costs that they are forced to pay. Any other decision would increase their costs, and if maximum profits are zero, would force them to operate at a loss and to leave the market in the long run. Yet, if these spill-over effects are not taken into account, inefficient allocations of resources will result. The solution lies in getting private costs and benefits to correspond to their social counterparts.

Several methods have been suggested for internalizing these externalities. If private producers treat the environment as a supply of free resources, they will use them until their marginal products are zero. But if these resources do have some social value, they should not be despoiled by being used for purposes that add less to public welfare than they cost. Privatization of common resources has already been considered as a possible solution to this problem. However, in many situations the technology to enforce ownership claims simply does not exist or their enforcement could be achieved only at resource cost that would exceed any potential benefit.

When the creation of property rights is not efficient, it is sometimes possible to simulate the workings of competitive markets. Even though market prices for particular resources may not be established, it may sometimes be possible to construct a system of taxes and fees that accomplishes essentially the same thing that better defined property rights might have accomplished. The important thing is to find a way, through penalty or subsidy, to remove the divergence between private and social costs and benefits. The ultimate problem, of course, is an informational one: how are we to measure social costs and benefits when they differ from observable market prices?

Once the optimal level of pollution has been identified, it should be possible to find a tax (to be levied on effluents) that would encourage an efficient allocation of pollution allotments to each effluent producer. The strategy is deceptively simple. Once the proper tax is imposed, polluters will have to decide whether to pay it or to reduce their effluent production. In the attempt to maximize profits, each firm will solve this problem in the least costly way. The polluters who can reduce their pollution most cheaply will do so, while the others will choose to pay the tax.

As long as firms cannot affect the tax rate, they will engage in pollution abatement until the marginal cleanup cost exactly equals the tax rate. If all firms face the same tax rate, this will lead to the satisfaction of the efficiency requirement that the marginal production cost of any particular commodity (a cleaner environment in this case) must be equal across all producers of that commodity. Two problems arise: (1) what is the optimal level of pollution? and (2) what is the proper tax rate?

We have already seen that the optimal level of pollution is not unique. It depends on the distribution of income. The determination of the proper tax rate is equally complex. If the government decides simply to make an initial guess and then to adjust the rate once it has observed producers' responses and measured their effect on environmental quality, the government can have no guarantees of actual improvement on the original failed market result. A critical problem is that the proper technique for pollution abatement depends on the amount of abatement in which the firm intends to engage. There probably are economies of scale in pollution abatement. However, if the government keeps changing the tax rate (and therefore the optimal amount of pollution abatement), any firm will always be cleaning up its waste at inefficient levels and with inefficient techniques.

Subsidies might provide a mechanism to compensate the producers of positive externalities. Again, of course, there are the twin problems of determining the output level where (unobservable) marginal social benefit equals (also unobservable) marginal social cost and what the appropriate subsidy rate should be. A particular case is the subsidy for education. Education has a number of important consequences, not the least of which is increased potential productivity. Through education, individuals develop human capital. Just as any other sort of economic capital, human capital is a produced means of production. Its production consumes resources (at the very least, the labor power lost while the person was spending time getting educated); once produced, it can be used in the production of other goods and services.

However, unlike other forms of capital, human capital is inalienable. For this reason, it is sometimes difficult to borrow the funds to finance education. Unlike other forms of capital, the lending institution cannot legally "repossess" human capital in case of default. This tends to make the cost of financing human capital greater than the cost of financing other types of capital and leads to a violation of our efficiency conditions. Because of the difference in the extent of property rights (and not because of any difference in their productivities), a bias against the production of human capital exists.

Education subsidies are one way to reduce the cost of human capital formation. There are, of course, other reasons for subsidizing education. If education makes one a better socialized individual, behavior presumably will be more predictable to others who experienced a similar socialization. This tends to reduce the uncertainties associated with social and economic interactions and ought therefore to further them. Others in society may benefit, but it is a benefit for which the educated person cannot charge. Anyone who must bear the full cost of education and who does not receive the full benefit will tend to underconsume. Education subsidies are intended to reduce the private cost of education and, therefore, to correct such underconsumption.

Government Intervention

We have seen how markets might fail to exploit fully all the opportunities for economic gain that arise from the possibilities of specialization and exchange. We have also seen how markets might fail to provide signals that, while leading to economically efficient resource allocation strategies, are consistent with societal norms of justice or equity. Quite frequently, such failures are the result of interdependencies between individuals that somehow fall outside the purview of existing market channels.

It sometimes is possible to redefine markets that fail or to simulate the conditions that would make them function efficiently. All this requires action by a decisionmaker whose scope transcends the more narrowly defined markets which, if allowed to continue to operate independently, will fail to take fully into account their interdependencies. Government might well be such a decisionmaker, since it ultimately defines the characteristics of the markets that exist.

Optimal Intervention Part of the beauty of unregulated markets is the efficiency with which they respond to changing conditions. In a static world it would be only a matter of time before some beneficent planner could, at least in principle, collect all the data necessary to allocate efficiently resources to production processes in a way that would maximize social welfare. Once the solution to the economic problem had been found, it could simply be implemented, and there would be no further need for markets (or even for planners).

Ours, however, is a world of constant flux. As soon as a solution to a problem has been found, the problem tends to change. This, of course, makes the old solution irrelevant at best. Rather than constructing a once-and-for-all plan, our planner would now have to be constantly in search of changed data. And whenever the data (taste and preferences, resource availabilities, and technological conditions) changed, the planner would have to readjust the plans. Any comprehensive planning would obviously consume a tremendous volume of resources.

This realization, that government intervention is itself resource consuming, suggests that we can reasonably seek the optimal level of intervention. Intervention ought to be carried out to the level where its marginal cost (in terms of resources required or efficiency forgone) has risen to the marginal social value of the intervention.

Practical Limitations While the optimal level of government intervention and regulation is easy to specify in principle, it may not be so simple to identify in practice. Since a significant part of most instances of market failure results from a divergence between private and social costs and benefits, to rectify the problem we must have some notion of what these generally nonobservable social costs and benefits might be. To the extent that this is not possible, the determination of optimal intervention levels is impossible.

An equally serious obstacle involves the motivation of political decisionmakers. We presume that government bureaucrats and legislators are also interested in making themselves as well off as possible, given the constraints under which they operate. If we assume that citizens are the principals in the governmental process and that the legislators are the agents, it should become immediately apparent that principal-agent problems can arise quite easily. The critical problem in establishing proper government machinery is the construction of incentives that minimize these problems.

SUMMARY

Because resources exist only in finite quantity, economic decisionmaking involves the allocation of those resources. Left to themselves, free markets allocate resources in the most efficient manner. An efficient allocation exists when any further attempt at improvement would result in more losses than gains. Consumers pay prices that reflect the rate at which they are willing to substitute one commodity for another. Producers hire factors at rates that maximize profits and therefore minimize costs. In the long run, however, the opportunity for profit brings new producers into the market, driving down the price until profits disappear. At that point, producers produce at the lowest cost possible, and consumers gain the greatest satisfaction possible given the resources available. The normal adjustments of free markets tend toward such maximum technical efficiency.

However, there are several possible reasons that markets might fail to yield efficient outcomes. When economies of scale, transaction costs, or collusion create market power, producers may restrict output and increase prices. Externalities, such as industrial accidents and pollution, can induce decisionmakers to produce more than the socially optimal level because they avoid some of the costs of production. If externalities deny them the full benefit of their efforts, they may produce too little or, in the extreme case of public goods, not at all. Efficient markets require all participants to have complete information, but many transactions occur in the midst of uncertainty or over such a long period of time that values may change. Markets either discount such factors or incorporate them through insurance mechanisms. Even the efficiency of insurance, however, can be undermined by moral hazard and adverse selection. When a principal acts in the market through an agent, the actions of the agent can be influenced by self-interest as well as the principal's interests. Finally, the outcome of the market always depends on the particular pattern of income distribution. At different income levels, people make different choices, but the appropriate distribution of income is primarily a question of equity rather than efficiency.

When markets fail to yield the best outcomes, different approaches to corrective action are possible. One approach attempts to redefine the market so that it allocates resources in a more acceptable manner. The objective is to eliminate the divergence between private costs and social costs. Extending property rights can have this effect because it requires those who wish to use resources to pay the owners for the right instead of consuming resources for free. Taxes and subsidies can also be used to internalize costs and benefits that would otherwise escape the market. A second approach to correcting market failures involves government intervention. The government can prescribe certain desired outcomes that free markets might not otherwise reach. While some level of government intervention may be necessary, there are practical limitations to the government's ability to regulate the economy efficiently. For this reason, the next chapter probes the challenges of regulation in economic decisionmaking.

CHAPTER 5

Economic Regulation

INTRODUCTION

The story of economics is frequently told in terms of perfectly competitive markets and the invisible hand. The invisible hand, however, does not necessarily lead to either efficient or socially desirable results. In some cases we therefore rely on the government— federal, state, and local—to restructure various aspects of the economic environment. The government is always in a position to change the outcome of individual actions. We hope it often improves the outcome.

According to a prominent economist, "No business, large or small, can operate without a myriad of government rules and restrictions. Costs and profits can be affected as much by a directive written by a government official as by a management decision in the front office or a customer's decision at the checkout counter."[1] Government regulation of business controls market behavior, employee relations, product design, advertising, environmental impacts, and a host of other corporate activities. During the 1960s and 1970s, Congress enacted over 100 laws regulating business activity. A variety of federal agencies as well as organs of state and local government also make regulations affecting business firms.

In addition to government regulations affecting business generally, certain industries must abide by specific regulations applying to that industry. Prominent examples of regulated industries are public utilities, transportation, broadcasting, insurance, and banking. Specific industries may be regulated at either the federal or state level, or sometimes both. Congress established the Interstate Commerce Commission in 1887, for example, because states were unable to regulate railroads operating in other states as well. Public utilities, on the other hand, usually operate in a limited area suitable to state regulation, although some aspects of their business may also fall under the control of federal agencies, such as the Nuclear Regulatory Commission.

The motivation for regulation can range from the entirely pure to the totally corrupt. History records instances at each extreme and many in between. Government power can easily be used to protect or increase the economic profits of those who have the ear of legislators.

REASONS FOR REGULATION

In a sense, the government regulates all aspects of our existence. It is the government, after all, that writes and enforces the laws of the land. Only periodically is the public explicitly asked to validate government public decisions at the ballot box. Citizens frequently organize along lines of special interests and try to influence the government decisions that particularly affect those special interests.

Although the American tradition of economic liberalism suggests that markets should be left to themselves, there are instances when the scope of government economic activity can be extended beyond the enforcement of private property and contract rights. For example, there are times when the extension of private property or contract rights is either not technologically feasible or when such extensions, while feasible, would consume far too many resources. These cases of market failure may justify specific government regulation. Institutional needs such as a sound financial system may require government control. In other instances, social objectives may be the motive for specific government regulation.

Market Failure

A system of competitive markets provides an extremely efficient coordinating device for the myriad of decisions made by interdependent individuals. Markets establish prices, which are then interpreted by economic agents as signals of relative scarcity. As long as prices truly reflect relative scarcity, and as long as there are no problems with the distribution of property rights, the self-interest of consumers and producers allocates scarce resources to their competing uses and regulates the distribution of that output to consumers in an efficient way.

Chapter 4 demonstrated that when markets are not competitive and prices fail to reflect relative scarcity, distortions arise in the allocation of resources. Noncompetitive markets can allocate resources, but the resulting allocation is usually inefficient. Information problems, externalities, and economies of scale often lead to regulation because the market allocation in such circumstances is inefficient.

Markets often fail to allocate resources efficiently when the *information* on which decisions are based is inaccurate or incomplete or where the acquisition of information is extremely difficult or costly. Some decisions made at one time cannot be easily reversed at a later time. Decisions made infrequently allow little opportunity for learning from one's mistakes. While in principle a system of taxes and subsidies could correct some of these problems, many of them are instead addressed by regulation. The Consumer Product Safety Commission, for example, through its labeling and testing efforts tries to inform consumers of some of the possible consequences of consuming certain products. Furthermore, the Commission tries to keep products it considers dangerous off the market.

The Food and Drug Administration and the Department of Agriculture pursue similar efforts. Regulators at these agencies inspect and test most of the food and drugs consumed by Americans. They evaluate the safety and purity of food and drugs. They inform the public of these results through an elaborate system of labels and the publication of extensive data bases.

A second type of market failure arises from *externalities*. Not all the costs or benefits associated with particular market decisions are incurred by or accrue to the decisionmakers. Producers and consumers in markets with significant externalities cannot take them into consideration even if they want to. While a few companies may destroy our environment because their management is extremely greedy or callous, even the firms that wish to act responsibly cannot afford to do so. In a competitive environment producers must cut their costs of production to the bone if they wish to earn their maximum profit. Now imagine that the corporation has the opportunity to use a resource such as clean river water for free for example. Management might well find it offensive to pollute the water. But if the industry is indeed competitive, if the cleanup of the water is costly, and if the firm's competitors do not feel the same compulsion to clean up their pollution (and voluntarily incur the cleanup costs) then management will eventually be forced out of business unless it avoids all the avoidable costs of pollution control.

Only if the costs of pollution are internalized through effluent charges, public censure, or regulation will management of competitive firms have even the option to be environmentally "responsible." The Environmental Protection Agency, because it can impose fines on violators, is able to enforce a set of standards designed to provide substitutes for what the market itself does not seem to do well. Although this agency has had some success in restoring the quality of some of our natural resources or at least in slowing the rate of degradation, serious questions have been brought to light concerning the cost at which these improvements were obtained. Two questions are often voiced: (1) was the particular objective attained at the lowest possible resource cost? and (2) did the marginal benefits of the project outweigh these minimum resource costs?

A third major source of market failure is the existence of significant *economies of scale.* When such economies exist and are not exhausted in plant sizes that are relatively small compared to the market demand for the commodity, the industry will be dominated by a small number of participants. Simply enforcing the antitrust laws and breaking up the firm or firms in such an industry will not be efficient. Forcing individual firms to operate on uneconomically small scales would be extremely wasteful of society's scarce resources.

It would be wasteful if we decreed that businesses would not be allowed to take full advantage of economies of mass production or specialization. The ultimate goal is not competitive markets per se. What we really want is a system for organizing production and distribution efficiently. When there are few producers in a market, however, the full force of competition is not likely to be brought to bear on market participants, and prices will tend to deviate from marginal cost. This discrepancy between marginal cost and price creates an inefficiency in the economy. The objective of a significant amount of regulation is to rectify this problem.

Financial Stability

In order to take full advantage of potential economies of scale and specialization, a modern economy must have some special institutions to facilitate the many and complex exchanges that must take place. Without exchange, specialization would not be possible, and we would be forced to consume significantly fewer goods and services. The most efficient method for transacting the business of society is to have some monetary system.

In order for an economy with a monetary system to work well, it must have certain characteristics. It is the very nature of monetary exchange that causes a time delay between the moment that useful goods and services are delivered and the moment that other useful goods and services are obtained. A critical characteristic of money, therefore, is that the type of future transaction it allows must be predictable. If we are not sure exactly what the purchasing power of our money will be when we decide to use it, we would not be inclined to exchange our goods and services for it. The exchange system would break down, and we would be forced into self-sufficient production or barter. In either case, the economic cost would be horrendous. For this reason, financial institutions play an important role in our economy. By supporting a monetary system that allows the ready exchange of monetary assets between individuals, financial institutions greatly increase the efficiency with which the economy operates. However, since most of the money we own exists only as claims against some financial institution, it is essential that we know for sure that these institutions will continue to exist, or that, in the event of a failure, we can assert our financial claims against some successor institution. Banks and insurance companies are examples of financial institutions.

The importance of a sound insurance system lies in its ability to transfer risk from policyholders. Without such a mechanism, many individuals would not dare to engage in activity that held a potential for loss. As a result, the vitality of the economic system would be severely reduced, and our standard of living would decline. Since finance and insurance play such major roles in the modern economy, their performance is always a matter of concern. Whenever problems are perceived in these industries, the instinctive reaction of society seems to be to tighten regulation. However, efforts to regulate the safety and soundness of these industries have imposed costs on the economy, while their benefits in terms of a sounder financial or insurance system have been uncertain.

Social Objectives

In addition to the economic objectives of technical and allocative efficiency and of a sound and stable financial system, there is yet another set of motivations for the regulation of economic activity. Frequently the wisdom of individuals does not accord with the wisdom of those in a position to impose their wills. The institutionalization of "social objectives" can often be interpreted as an attempt by one group of individuals, legislators, or their advisers, to supplant the wisdom of some with their own more "responsible" judgments. For a variety of reasons, individuals have different levels of appreciation for particular goods and services. Children, for example, are not usually known for their love of going to school. Even their parents are sometimes not fully convinced of the benefits of schooling and might prefer instead to find their child a paying job. This preference might be even more likely if the family does not have much income. However, since education usually is considered to be in the interest of society, the law requires all children to attend school until at least age sixteen. Furthermore, in order to reduce the potential for economic exploitation of children, the law severely limits the employment opportunities of children. (This limitation is another instance of an externality.)

Another major reason for regulation is the desire to alter the distribution of income. Despite all the efficiency characteristics of competitive or nearly competitive market results, nothing in economic theory suggests that the resulting distribution of income is optimal, or even desirable.

One of the measures of a civilized society surely is the way it provides for those who, for whatever reason, cannot or will not on their own provide themselves with some minimum standard of living. Two issues stand out. First, there is the notion that individuals should have an equal opportunity to provide for themselves. All citizens should have the choice to use their skills. Most skills, however, are not innate; they are developed. Skills—whether mental or physical—are the result of training and investment. However, as with all kinds of investment, it is a costly and time-consuming process. Equal opportunity to earn a living must include an equal opportunity to invest in skill development if it is not to become an empty slogan.

The second issue is poverty. Our analysis started with the assumption of a *given* distribution of endowments, but nothing can be deduced about the correctness of such an initial endowment. The market structure and economic environment depend on the original distribution of resources. The final distribution of income would be different if the original endowment of resources had been largely in the hands of baseball fans instead of opera lovers. The relative incomes of baseball players and opera stars would depend on the distribution, and the extent to which the market would cater to the tastes and preferences of these resource suppliers would also be affected.

Another social objective is stabilization policy. Certain sectors of the economy are more resistant to the strains of economic fluctuations than are other sectors. Regulation of the level of economic activity is partly designed to smooth out the peaks and valleys, the abrupt swings. Much of the regulatory framework for banks and other financial institutions was originally designed to increase the stability of the system.

REGULATION OF IMPERFECT MARKETS

Differing conditions and technologies allow for the development of industries that are organized in radically different ways. When entry into an industry is extremely easy or nearly costless, and when exit from the industry is equally easy and does not involve the writing off of large investment, the industry tends to be competitive. When legal barriers, such as regulatory standards for the product, or economic barriers, such as significant economies of scale, restrict entry, the industry might have only a single firm. While these two extremes are useful benchmarks for measuring the benefits of competition or, more particularly, the costs of deviation from competition, they leave something to be desired as descriptions of the real world. Very little economic activity in this country is carried out under conditions of perfect competition or monopoly. The very term monopolist is somewhat misleading because its applicability always depends on the way in which we choose to define the market under study. Campbell Soup clearly has a monopoly in the Campbell Soup market, but because of reasonably good canned and packaged substitutes, it can hardly be accused of having a monopoly or even a near monopoly in the prepared soup market. Once we broaden our concept of the relevant market to the market for food products, Campbell Soup becomes an almost inconsequential agent.

The same argument holds to varying degrees for most monopolists. Even an electric utility—one of the most obviously monopolistic firms—does not face a completely inelastic demand for its output. While televisions do not run well on gasoline, gasoline-powered generators could produce enough electricity to power our appliances. The reason we do not rely on gasoline generators (except in emergencies or in wilderness areas) is that they are uneconomical. However, if the electric utility were to increase its rates enough, we might find it cheaper to generate our electricity at home. Large corporations have already discovered that it sometimes pays them to generate electricity along with the power needed for the normal production process and to sell the excess electricity back to the electric company.

Regulation of Market Power

The essential attribute of market power is that the consumer has no ready substitute for the product. As long as the consumer cannot substitute one commodity for another, the producer is free to raise the price. A profit-maximizing producer sets its price at a level so that marginal cost equals marginal revenue. The extent to which marginal revenue deviates from price is a function of the degree of the market power. Under perfect competition, where the producer does not have any market power, there is no divergence between marginal revenue and price. For this reason, marginal cost will equal price—exactly the condition for allocative efficiency.

As economists or as consumers, we might decry the divergence between marginal revenue and price as a sign of an inefficient allocation of resources. Under some fairly general conditions, a divergence between price and marginal cost implies that the economy as a whole is operating at an interior point in its production possibilities set. This suggests that we are living with economically unnecessary scarcity. The average standard of living could be improved if we removed the source of this inefficiency—market power.

Of course, a producer would have a completely different point of view. It would clearly be to the producer's advantage if the degree of competition in the output market were reduced. The greater the degree of market power, the more the producer can raise the price above marginal cost and increase profits.

More than two centuries ago, Adam Smith observed that only rarely do businessmen get together for any purpose other than to conspire against the general public. The results of such conspiracies are always the same—to increase the profits of the sellers by restricting competition. The methods used almost always involve fixing prices or restricting output. While there are some industries, the natural monopolies and perhaps the natural oligopolies, where the economies of scale are such as to make smaller scale production inefficient, society usually is served better if competition is not restricted. However, producers in all industries would find it potentially advantageous to limit competition.

Under conditions of perfect competition, it is almost impossible to restrict competition, except through government edict or private force. New competitors enter the industry when there appear to be positive profits earned by incumbents. Potential competitors are quite literally waiting in the wings, ready to take away whatever profit opportunities exist. An incumbent supplier is free to raise prices at any time, but when prices rise above marginal cost, a potential competitor will become an actual competitor and steal customers by selling to them at a lower price. The best course is either trying to keep these potential competitors out of the market altogether, or if they wish to enter, to keep them from cutting their prices. In other words, it is in a firm's best interest to try to restrain trade. The antitrust laws of this country can be seen, at least in part, as a response to this natural tendency for businesses to conspire to restrain trade.

However, there might be some real benefits attached to imperfectly competitive market structures. Economies of scale and specialization should be fully exploited if the economy is to put its scarce resources to their most productive uses, but it is possible that there are also some other benefits. The rigors of competition, in particular the inability to earn economic profits, might make investments in research and development—particularly in basic research—a risky venture. Some evidence suggests that large oligopolists sometimes devote considerable resources to basic research, such as AT&T's Bell Labs. Of course, for each of these examples there is a counter example. One reason for the poor competitive position of the U.S. steel industry in world markets may be that the industry failed to divert any significant portion of its oligopoly profits into research and development and now finds itself technologically disadvantaged.

There are significant externalities involved in the introduction of new technology. Patent law can never fully guarantee that all benefits arising from an invention will accrue to the inventor, even for an eighteen-year period. If one firm, however, engages in most of the production in the industry where the new discovery is likely to be useful, then it can capture a greater portion of the benefit than would be possible in a dispersed production environment where the benefits would accrue largely to the other market participants. This greater certainty of capturing the benefits of improved technology makes investments in basic research more attractive for industrial giants with a significant market share.

If one of the major sources of problems that might arise in a market economy is the concentration of economic power, what better way to deal with it than to prevent such power from arising to begin with or to break it up once it has been observed to exist. If we could structure the legal system in such a way as to outlaw market power, then it would seem that the problem might be solved. This has been the rationale behind the antitrust laws of the United States.

Notice that there are really several issues involved here. The type of action considered an exercise of market power needs to be defined, and the extent of market power needs to be measured. Corrective action depends on the ability to identify clearly any act of market power. If this were possible, transgressors could be fined or sanctioned. It also would help to measure the propensity for market power or the potential market power of a firm.

Since monitoring is a resource-consuming activity, every economic activity cannot be monitored for potential violations of law. However, there is an incentive structure to encourage victims to report violators. The Sherman Act provides for treble damage awards (three times the amount of the demonstrable damages) to the plaintiff in a civil suit brought against an entity found guilty of price fixing. Such illegal activities are more likely to be spotted by those against whom they are perpetrated. In addition, with the possibility of recovery of treble damages, the victims have a real interest in reporting any violations to the proper authorities.

Also advantageous would be some relatively simple signals to indicate where closer inspection would most likely reveal prosecutable offenses. This was the notion behind *concentration ratios*. The belief was that if a small number of firms sold a significant portion of the total industry output, at least the appearance of market power existed. However, this reliance on measures of the relative size of actual members of the industry has recently come under attack. Economists and some regulators have come to realize that the number of firms in the industry is not nearly as important as is the ease of entry into the industry. For example, suppose there is only one firm active in the industry. Those who emphasize concentration ratios would immediately spring into action; the concentration ratio could not possibly get any higher. Others would be more interested in the degree to which the market is contestable. The single supplier would still not have any market power if, whenever he raised price above marginal cost, new firms would immediately start up and steal away his customers. Thus, despite the fact that concentration ratios are measurable and can provide quantifiable benchmarks, great care must be taken in interpreting them as prima facie evidence of market power.

Concentration of Industry If perfect competition requires a large number of firms, each so small it cannot impose its will on the market, then the opposite of competitive conditions allows a few large firms to dominate the market. Firms that supply a significant portion of their respective markets frequently have some power to influence the terms and conditions of trade in those markets. For example, their refusal to expand output could lead to shortages that make price increases possible.

History records several periods in American history when significant concentrations of industry have occurred. During the 1890s the number of firms fell sharply. Significant concentrations of firms arose in several industries. The 1920s also saw a movement toward concentration. The 1960s witnessed a period of conglomerate mergers. Again the number of independent business entities dropped.

But does a smaller number of firms automatically mean less competition? Actually, all three of these major merger periods occurred at times when there were significant improvements in transportation or communication technology. Since both transportation and communication reduce the friction of distance, these developments should have increased the degree of competition, all other things being equal. If transportation costs are high, for example, the effective market area for most producers will be fairly small. As transportation costs fall, the market area in which the delivered price makes the commodity saleable increases. But this means that the market power of local firms shrinks as foreign producers begin to invade the local market. This is what happened in the last decades of the nineteenth century as the railroad system was put into place. It happened again in the 1960s when the interstate highway system was constructed. The 1920s, of course, saw major improvement in communication technology with the development of the radio and the popularization of the telephone.

We can discern several distinct types of merger activity. *Vertical integration* occurs when one firm gains control of another firm in the same industry but located at a different point in the production process. One firm acquires either a supplier of its inputs or a purchaser of its output such as, for example, an oil refiner purchasing retail gasoline outlets or oil drilling facilities. Vertical integration is not necessarily inefficient. Most firms are vertically integrated to some degree since most production processes involve sequential steps. To the extent that complete specialization is unwarranted, any sequence of production activities could be considered an example of vertical integration.

When control over a stage of the production process leads to economic power over competitors somewhere else in the production chain, however, vertical integration becomes pernicious. One firm that controls an essential raw material, for example, can dominate all markets farther down the chain toward the ultimate consumer. By instituting appropriate pricing policies for the sale of the raw material, that firm can effectively dictate the cost structure, and therefore the profitability, of competitors at later stages in the production process.

Horizontal integration restricts the number of competitors in a specific market. If one firm can gain control over competing firms through direct acquisition of their assets or control of the decisionmaking power, it can stop these competitors from eroding its profits by undercutting prices. Without competitors, it can set price or output levels so as to maximize monopoly profits. Unless there are some significant, unexploited economies of scale or scope, both vertical and horizontal mergers tend to lessen competition. They are therefore severely restricted by the Sherman Act and the Clayton Act.

The case against *conglomerate mergers* is not always as clear. A conglomerate merger is a combination of firms in unrelated industries. It is not immediately clear, therefore, how such combinations restrain trade or otherwise lead to a lessening of competition. Most of the criticism of conglomerate mergers arises from the perceived social and political implications of such mergers. There is often a profound antipathy toward the sheer size of a business. The bigger the business, the more outlets for the opinions and prejudices of the decisionmakers. Management of a corporation with 50,000 employees has a large, interested audience for its political opinion. Since most of these employees are also voters, some observers fear that management can exert undue influence in the political process.

Another fear is that conglomerate mergers can produce firms with such great financial strength that they can create artificial barriers to entry. If a firm had sufficient financial resources, it could conceivably use this strength to engage in predatory pricing. *Predatory pricing* occurs when one firm sells its output at prices that fail to cover costs in an attempt to bankrupt the competition. The firm that can run at a loss the longest will survive this war and can then, as the only survivor in the market, raise prices and extract monopoly profits. The critics of conglomerate mergers argue that corporate giants are the most likely practitioners of predatory pricing, at the expense of smaller local or regional firms.

Antitrust Law   Evaluating the antitrust laws as a means for reducing the undesirable effects of imperfect competition requires more than a simple reading of the law. The impact of a law depends not only on what it says but also on how it is interpreted and enforced. A law that says it is illegal to hunt game without a license, but which is not enforced (for example, because there is no provision for the hiring of game wardens) is not likely to be effective. Similarly, a law that says "all men" are to be treated equally before the law can be interpreted at one time to deny such rights to women and interpreted at another time to guarantee such rights to all without regard to race, gender, or religion.

The Sherman Antitrust Act of 1890 marked an important milestone in the growing involvement of the federal government in determining or attempting to determine the structure of and the conduct in many different markets in the U.S. In response to a growing clamor by farmers, small businesses, and others who found themselves disadvantaged by the behavior of large corporations, Congress empowered the Antitrust Division of the Justice Department to put an end to conspiracies to restrain trade and to the attempts of firms to monopolize their markets. Section 1 of the Sherman Act provides penalties for firms and their officers convicted of making contracts or agreements or of engaging in conspiracies to fix prices, output levels, or other factors that lessen or otherwise impede trade in this country or internationally. While the intent of the act seems reasonably clear, attempts at its enforcement through the court system have revealed some problems of interpretation or measurement.

The U.S. Supreme Court consistently has held that the existence of a contract or documented agreement in which the parties agree to lessen competition is a clear violation of the act. The interpretive problem arises with respect to the definition of a conspiracy. Unless the conspirators have carelessly committed their illegal activities to paper, the existence of conspiracies is difficult to demonstrate. Usually the only evidence is an observation that certain activities of different individuals are too similar to have resulted without explicit coordination.

The issue of conspiracy is probably the most difficult when there is only a small group of producers. Informal agreements between these "competitors" are reached easily, especially if the resulting pricing, output, or market-sharing policies benefit all parties. Yet, these agreements are difficult to discover. *Collusion* can take many forms. An easy, but difficult to discern, method of collusion occurs when one firm sets the joint monopoly profit maximizing price, and all other firms follow its "leadership" role. While *price leadership* is an effective collusive device, and despite the fact that similar prices are easy to detect, the courts have not tended to convict only for this reason. There has been some tendency, however, to convict if the pricing similarities appear to be overly profuse—if the "parallelism of action" is too great.

The Clayton Act of 1914 strengthened the prohibition of market power abuse. It brought into sharper focus precisely what kinds of activities were to be interpreted as restraints of trade. The Clayton Act specifically made *price discrimination* and tying contracts illegal.

Market power exists when a firm's customers do not have readily available substitutes. Of course, not all customers are the same, and certain customers have fewer real options than others. Particularly smaller customers in more isolated areas are likely to have fewer substitutes available to them than larger customers in better served markets. A firm discriminates when it segregates different types of customers according to their ability to substitute and charges them different prices not because they can be served only at different costs, but because they have fewer options from which to choose.

Tying contracts allow customers to purchase particular goods and services only in conjunction with the purchase of some other good or service. If a dairy firm forces its independent distributors, for example, to buy overpriced refrigeration units before selling them extremely popular ice cream, it would be in violation of the Clayton Act.

The provisions against price discrimination and tying contracts were intended to outlaw practices that tended to reduce competition. Closely related in intent was the provision of the Clayton Act that made interlocking directorates illegal and prevented companies from taking over competitors by buying their stock. Such activity was deemed conducive to the development of monopoly power because it made cooperation between rivals much easier. Certainly, if Company A controls most of the voting stock or directors of Company B, and therefore effectively has control over Company B's managers' employment contracts, it is much more likely that Company A and Company B will be able to agree on some amicable division of the market and any potential monopoly profits.

Various parts of the Clayton Act were amended during the century. The Celler-Kefauver Act of 1954 made mergers that tend to lessen competition more difficult. Companies had evaded the provisions of the Clayton Act by directly acquiring the assets of their competitors, rather than just the stock owner claims against these assets. The Celler-Kefauver Act closed this particular loophole. The Federal Trade Commission Act of 1914 also strengthened the laws against anticompetitive practices. The Federal Trade Commission (FTC), although probably not terribly effective during its first few decades, has recently become one of the more powerful weapons in the federal antitrust arsenal. Like the Antitrust Division of the Justice Department, the FTC is empowered to bring suit against violators under the Sherman and Clayton Acts. In addition to this power, the FTC has certain powers usually associated with the courts. It can, for example, investigate certain activities and then issue a cease-and-desist order against the offenders. Subject to judicial review, the FTC can act as prosecutor and judge, particularly in cases of unfair competition.

For almost the entire history of antitrust law in the United States, the emphasis has been on forestalling anticompetitive behavior. The courts have ruled certain actions to be illegal, but have never gone so far as to rule it illegal to be a monopoly. Attitudes toward monopoly and oligopoly have varied over the years. The "rule of reason" doctrine at the beginning of the century held that as long as the conduct was reasonable, large firms should not be prosecuted for sheer size. The New Deal and World War II era shifted the emphasis to structure rather than performance (Alcoa Aluminum was found to be in violation of the Sherman Act because it controlled 90 percent of its market, although it had engaged in no illegal activities to obtain such a large market share). The Reagan administration resumed the reluctance to bring suit against companies simply because of their market dominance.

Monopoly Regulation

While many economists think that regulating potentially competitive industries is inefficient, such concern does not extend to the regulation of monopolies. There is an extensive body of economic literature that addresses the distortion caused by monopolistic behavior. Precisely because monopolistic behavior tends to create inefficiencies, there is room for regulatory activity to improve the workings of an unregulated market. As long as the resources required by the regulatory process can generate benefits that exceed the value of their next best alternative employment, it pays for society to try to obtain the potential gains from allocative efficiency that monopolists intentionally fail to exploit. Of course, the very act of regulation can lead to inefficiency. To the extent that these inefficiencies plus the resource cost of regulation itself might offset the potential gains from regulation, there are some economists who would minimize even the regulation of monopolies.

Examples of the advantages and disadvantages of regulation can be found in the regulation of public utilities. Electric utilities are generally believed to be subject to increasing returns to scale. Thus it would be inefficient to divide the industry into many small, competing firms. However, if a single firm could select price and output in whatever way it pleased, the allocative inefficiencies associated with monopoly pricing would result. For this reason, we allow a utilities commission to supervise the rate-setting and output determination processes of an electric utility. One of the problems for regulatory agencies, however, is that the courts have ruled that regulated utilities must be allowed to earn a "fair" rate of return on their properly undertaken investment. The fair rate of return usually lies somewhere between the unregulated monopoly rate of return and the firm's cost of capital. The fact that the allowed rate of return tends to exceed the firm's cost of capital gives the regulated firm an incentive to overinvest in physical capital. If the firm builds too many additional plants, it is no longer producing at minimum cost—in other words, some of society's resources are being wasted.

Rate Regulation   If we examine the cost structure of a firm that has unexploited economies of scale throughout the range of relevant output levels, the problem can be grasped easily. The policy dilemma is this: if we were to force the firm to increase its output level until price no longer exceeded marginal cost, we would be forcing the firm to operate at an economic loss. Current interpretations of law would count this as an unconstitutional confiscation of private property. Regulators must either stop short of forcing the allocative solution approximating what would have resulted in a competitive environment, or they must be prepared to subsidize the economic losses with which they would have to burden the monopolist. Exhibit 5-1 illustrates the problem. If left alone, the monopolist would maximize profits by charging price P_1 and selling Q_1 units of output. Since price exceeds average cost, AC_1, the shaded area represents positive economic profits. From an economist's perspective, this solution also represents missed opportunities for expanding the value of society's output. If the rest of the economy were perfectly competitive, for example, consumers would value an extra unit of the monopolist's output at P_1 (since that is what they are willing to pay for it), while they value the next best use of the resources required to do this at only MC_1 (the marginal opportunity cost of the monopolist's output). There is the possibility for gain $(P_1 - MC_1)$ that is not being exploited.

If the government were to impose a ceiling price of P_2, all prices

Exhibit 5-1
Effects of Rate Regulation

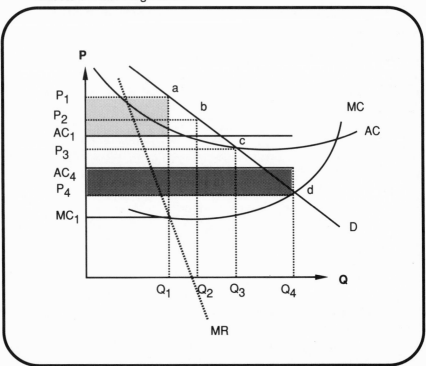

above P_2 (in particular, P_1) would be irrelevant because they are illegal. What would the monopolist do? First observe that the firm can earn a positive profit ($P_2 - AC_1$ per unit of output) by producing Q_1. However, at that point it is no longer maximizing its profit. Since it could certainly sell an additional unit of output at the price P_2, and since this is more than the marginal cost MC_1, profit would increase (by $P_2 - MC_1$) if the monopolist produced at least one additional unit. In fact, it would pay the monopolist to expand output all the way to Q_2.

This is precisely the logic behind rate regulation. As regulators set lower and lower price ceilings, the monopolist has an incentive to expand output (as long as marginal revenue continues to exceed marginal cost). The problem for the regulators is to discover just how low the regulated price can be set. If the regulators reduce the price all the way down to P_4, the monopolist would respond by producing Q_4 (assuming that all variable costs were covered), and price would equal marginal cost, exactly as desired. However, at Q_4, average total cost, AC_4, exceeds price, and the monopolist operates at an economic loss (the shaded area). Subsidizing the monopolist at taxpayer expense presents political difficulties. The most frequent solution to the problem is to get as close to the "competitive solution" (price equals marginal cost) as possible. In other words, rate regulators try to discover the lowest possible price that still allows the monopolist to avoid economic losses. P_3 is such a price. P_3, sometimes referred to as the *full cost price*, allows the monopolist a maximum profit of zero. Moreover, the only way to achieve zero profits is to produce Q_3 units of output. When the monopolist produces Q_3 units, price equals cost per unit, and economic profits are zero. At output levels above Q_3, price would be less than average total cost, and profits would therefore be negative.

Notice what rate regulation has accomplished. It has changed the monopolist's incentive structure so that its profit-maximizing decisions are closer to those that might have characterized competitive conditions. Rate regulation causes the monopolist to move from Point a on the demand curve to Point b, c, or d, depending on where the regulators set the ceiling. Point b still allows a profit, Point d leads to a loss, but Point c represents the full cost price. What has attracted many economists to this kind of regulatory scheme is that it relies on the profit-maximizing motives of the producer. There is no need to depend on the monopolist's social conscience or other lofty motives. In a proper pricing environment self-interest suffices to narrow the gap between price and marginal cost and to increase output levels.

While rate regulation with textbook diagrams must seem fairly simple, real world applications of the underlying principles are not nearly as neat. An immediate concern of regulators, for example, is the location of the cost and demand curves illustrated in Exhibit 5-1. It is one thing to assert that they exist; it is quite another to identify their parameters. The exact shape and location of the demand and cost curves are important in ratemaking because without them it would be impossible to set appropriate prices. If the demand had been greater than anticipated, P_3 would have resulted in positive economic profits. The price could have been set lower, and output could have expanded without forcing the monopolist to operate at a loss. It might seem that the regulator could simply wait for profits to be reported and then continue to lower the allowed rate until the profit disappeared. That approach, however, creates a perverse incentive. If the monopolist knows that the regulated price and profits will be reduced when it reports positive profits, its incentive is to avoid profit. It is a well-known fact in industry that it is much easier to reduce positive profits than to reduce losses. All one has to do is increase the cost of production. Ways to increase the cost of doing business can include raising salaries, purchasing additional office equipment, and increasing staff.

In a competitive environment, such practices would not work unless these expenses were truly necessary. Some competitor would surely have better budgetary controls, and these lower costs could help to drive the high-cost producer out of business. It is in the best interest of a competitive firm to reduce costs to the bare minimum—in other words, to be efficient, but efficiency is not in the best interest of a regulated monopolist.

The regulators could impose strict standards of financial accounting and avoid most of the problem, but that is not so easy. One of the big problems is obtaining sufficient information and technical expertise. If the firm is a monopolist, there are no close competitors. Even if the monopoly is only regional, most of the people who have developed expertise in the industry tend to work for a regulated firm. Given that their employment opportunities lie largely within the industry, such experts are not inclined to squeeze excess profits out of the industry. Without the experts, however, it is difficult to distinguish between proper and improper expenses and costs.

Regulatory Agencies   Regulatory agencies charged with ensuring the soundness of an industry have often fallen into the trap of equating soundness with survival of all the members of the industry. This confusion has led to perverse rate regulation practices and has institutionalized inefficiencies. Rather than setting rates that are fully compensatory for firms that use the best available techniques, *best practice firms*, regulatory agencies and commissions have tended to set rates that are compensatory for the weakest, or *worst practice firms*.

Thus the emphasis on rates that allow the survival of all firms has removed the central motivating power of a market system—the fear of failure or bankruptcy. Under competitive conditions, management has no choice but to maximize profits. Any inefficiency will surely raise costs and result in economic losses. Even a monopolist, if the owners paid the discounted present value of future monopoly profits for the firm, will be forced to operate in a technically efficient way (albeit at a socially inefficient scale) if it is to avoid economic losses. However, a regulated firm, whose survival is essentially guaranteed by the regulatory agency, is under no such compulsion. In fact, it will be indifferent to the economic efficiency of its operation as long as it is guaranteed at least the market rate of return on all its expenditures.

This regulatory practice causes inefficiency because it removes the incentive, and certainly the necessity, for quick adaptation to changing market condition. In a fairly static economic environment, this result may not be of great consequence. Properly motivated regulators would probably discover inefficiencies in due time and could, in principle, regulate the conduct and performance of the firm so as to remove the inefficiencies. However, in times of rapidly changing markets or technology, the information lag tends to overload the regulators.

The Interstate Commerce Commission (ICC) was established in 1887 to regulate railroads. At that time many shippers felt that the regional monopoly power of the railroads was being exercised unfairly. The political power of agricultural interest was brought to bear on the economic decisions made by railroad executives. Even though its original intent was to protect shippers, however, the ICC very quickly became the protector of railroads.

While it became increasingly more difficult in other industries to fix prices, the rate-setting practices of the ICC quickly became little more than legalized price fixing. Since the railroads had such a well-focused interest in railroad tariffs, while shippers, especially the smaller ones, generally did not have the time or resources to participate in increasingly formal ratemaking procedures, the whole process tended to be skewed in favor of the railroads. When the trucking industry began to offer significant competition for freight transportation, the ICC rapidly moved to bring the trucking industry under its control. Few people would argue that there are significant economies of scale in the trucking industry. Yet, regulation was immediately imposed, not to control the destructive practices of a natural monopolist, but to prevent unconstrained competition with an industry already under ICC control. Rather than trying to discover ways in which transportation services could be delivered more efficiently, the ICC actively sought to prevent a large influx of low-cost competitors.

The Federal Communications Commission (FCC) took a similar approach. When technological change made long-distance voice and data communications possible without the complete dependence on a network of wires, other firms could offer AT&T some vigorous competition. As long as communications depended on the existence of a physical connection, the argument that the industry was a natural monopolist was persuasive. With the development of microwave and satellite communication links, the fixed capacity networks originally responsible for the economies of scale become far less critical in the delivery of an acceptable product. Instead of finding ways to integrate the new technology into the communications system, the FCC expended considerable resources to keep new competitors out of the industry.

Regulation Versus Nationalization The existence of natural monopolies usually means that there will be calls to "do something" about the behavior of unconstrained monopolists. In the United States the response to this call has frequently taken the form of a regulatory commission. The ICC regulates a considerable, although diminishing, portion of surface freight and passenger transportation. The FCC regulates radio, television, and voice and data communications. State public utilities commissions also regulate these industries as well as the electric and gas utilities.

Regulation by commission, however, is not the only way to deal with the problem. In many countries, for example, the government owns and operates the railroads. In the United States the federal government owns and operates the postal service. While many think that nationalized enterprise would never work in the United States, it does represent an alternative to regulation by commission. In fact, nationalized enterprises exist in many countries and to a greater extent in the U.S. than often realized. While many Americans would oppose nationalization of the railroads, for example, the industries against which they compete—truck, barge, pipeline, and air transportation—enjoy nationalized facilities. What makes the railroad a natural monopoly is not the trains that deliver the services; it is the track and terminal network over which they must operate. Since the investment in rights-of-way and structures is fixed, it presents a formidable barrier to entry. While all the competing modes also require a fixed terminal and "track system," considerable portions of their networks are actually owned and operated by governments.

The interstate highway system gives trucks an advantage over railroads in their competition for medium-distance freight. While trucks do pay fees for the use of these highways, most of the charge relates to the actual usage level, which varies from year to year because the transportation industry is quite cyclical. During lean years, trucks do not pay for the highways they do not use, while railroads must continue to pay for and maintain their trackage and rights-of-way.

The development of air travel benefited at least in part from technological externalities created by defense contracting. Another significant advantage for the airline industry is that government owns and operates most airports and controls the airways. Government agencies also provide navigation and weather information.

Water transportation also benefits from government-produced and -maintained navigable waterways and aids to navigation at little or no cost. While pipelines are heavily regulated, the production of gas and oil is subject to far less regulation. So nationalization of the infrastructure—the railroad tracks and switching yards—would have many parallels in the transportation industry and would remove a considerable source of the economies of scale that motivated the regulation of the railroad industry.

A similar approach might be taken to the problem of regulating the electric utilities. There is little evidence that the generation of electricity involves such extensive economies of scale as to preclude a significantly more competitive environment. The economies of scale arise mainly from the fixed distribution system. Another solution to the regulatory problem, then, might well consist of separating the distribution network from the production of power—much the same way that we have separated the operation of transportation networks from the operation of the vehicles that use them.

REGULATION OF FINANCIAL INSTITUTIONS

Financial institutions such as banks and insurance companies present some unique regulatory problems. Because financial institutions facilitate other business transactions, public confidence in them is essential if the economy is to function smoothly and efficiently. Yet the services they provide are often too complex for all consumers to analyze and compare readily. Thus significant information problems exist. Unless regulation prescribes some minimum requirements and standards, competition in a market with less than perfect information will favor firms tempted to engage in deceptive practices. For this reason, regulation serves the interest of the most reputable firms in the industry as much as it protects the public. Regulators must then decide, however, what practices are acceptable, and they may limit innovation as a result.

Financial institutions also enjoy significant economies of scale. The main reason that financial institutions exist is that they can process a large volume of transactions more efficiently than individuals. These economies of scale can be a source of market power. Competition might be limited because only certain firms have the expertise or the technology to operate efficiently.

Financial institutions also have a fiduciary responsibility because they hold other people's money. Financial transactions often involve long-term commitments, and conditions can change over that period. An inefficient financial institution may be unable to compete effectively and be forced out of business. Such market discipline promotes efficiency overall, but the customers of an insolvent financial institution are the real losers. To protect the public, regulations must either provide effective guarantee mechanisms or preserve the solvency of all firms. Regulators in both the banking and the insurance industries have struggled with these challenges.

Banking

The regulation of the banking industry has changed radically during the twentieth century. Before the Great Depression of the 1930s, there was relatively little special regulation of banking, especially at the federal level. Banking was an essentially competitive industry subject to the general regulatory authority of government. Banks competed for the available supply of funds and for the broad array of assets typically created by financial intermediaries.

The depression of the 1930s, which was in large part blamed on the failure of the banking system, significantly changed public attitudes toward banks. Critics blamed the collapse on the "excesses" of competition that had come to characterize the banking industry during the 1920s. Competition for deposits had led the banks to offer higher and higher interest rates, while as the cost of funds climbed, banks were forced to seek out assets with greater rates of return in order to protect their profitability. Since the effective rate of return on assets is usually a function of the riskiness of the investment, this phenomenon appeared to have forced banks to acquire ever more speculative assets. The economic collapse of the 1930s was widely attributed to this deterioration of the quality of the banking industry's asset portfolio.

Since a sound banking system is essential to the smooth operation of a complex market economy, the debacle of the 1930s convinced many observers that the banking industry was simply too important to be left on its own. In quick succession a series of new banking laws brought the industry under rather tight federal control. The Bank Acts of 1933 and 1935, the Securities Exchange Act of 1934, and various amendments to the Federal Reserve Act of 1913 changed the character of the industry. The primary objective of the regulation imposed during the 1930s was to ensure the soundness of the industry. The strategy for achieving that goal was to eliminate the type of competition thought to have destabilized the industry during the late 1920s. Competition for deposits was severely restricted by regulations limiting the interest rate banks could pay. Competition for assets was reduced by rules that prohibited or severely restricted the acquisition of speculative assets such as common equities or loans to developing nations. Competition was further reduced by clearly delineating different lending functions for different types of institutions. Partly through the use of the tax code, for example, commercial banks were discouraged from concentrating their portfolios in mortgage loans. In order to keep savings and loan associations focused on their primary mission, the granting of residential real estate mortgages, regulation did not allow them to make consumer loans or to issue credit cards. Although this regulatory environment limited bank flexibility, it did achieve its goal of creating and maintaining a sound banking system. As with most regulatory schemes, the process worked tolerably well as long as the economic environment was fairly static or changed in fairly predictable or controllable ways. When conditions began to change rapidly, as they did in the mid-to-late 1960s and 1970s, the inflexibility of regulation and the failure of regulators to adapt quickly caused severe dislocations in the industry.

The Depository Institutions Deregulation and Monetary Control Act of 1980 represented the first major attempt to restructure the banking industry since the 1930s. It sought to reverse the close regulation and anticompetitive restrictions instituted during the Great Depression. Rather than trying to ensure the soundness of the industry by reducing competition and attempting to guarantee the survival of all the firms in the industry, the new law relied on competitive prices to ensure the health of the industry. No longer did individual banks have their survival practically guaranteed. Only those banks that were well-managed and could stand up to the competition could survive. The others would be allowed to fall by the wayside. The free market would finally be allowed to do what it does best—force quick adaptation to changes in the economic environment.

The problems of certain major banks, however, showed that there are also limits to how far we can go in that direction. Competitive pressures caused banks to make riskier loans in the hope of generating higher returns. Government-arranged mergers and bailouts prevented the failure of several institutions that might have led to a financial panic. Neither government regulation nor market discipline seems to offer an absolute guarantee of bank solvency.

Insurance

Because insurance allows risk-averse individuals to substitute certain, or nearly certain, outcome for potential catastrophes, the ready availability of insurance is a necessary ingredient in the efficient operation of markets. Insurance promotes economic stability by helping markets capture the costs of uncertain events. Thus the stability of the insurers is all the more important.

State regulation of insurance began when state legislatures granted charters to new insurance companies and specified certain conditions regarding their minimum capital, their investments, and final disclosure. States subsequently levied premium taxes on insurers and required reports for that purpose. During the latter half of the nineteenth century, states established insurance departments to supervise the operations of insurance companies. As abuses received increasing attention, the emphasis of state regulation gradually shifted toward protection of the public. State law, for example, often prescribes standard contract language for certain lines of insurance. Under the laws of most states, state insurance commissioners have the authority to regulate rates, to promulgate rules, to enforce the state insurance laws, to intervene in disputes between insureds and insurers, to license insurers to transact business within the state, to examine the financial condition and market conduct of insurers, and to license agents and brokers.[2]

Before World War II, the Supreme Court consistently ruled that insurance was not interstate commerce, and therefore, it did not fall under the purview of the federal antitrust statutes. In 1944 the Supreme Court reversed this interpretation; it declared that insurance was, in fact, interstate commerce and that it should not be exempt from antitrust law. In order to forestall the impending emasculation of state regulations, Congress enacted the McCarran-Ferguson Act, which made it clear that regulatory authority over the insurance industry rested in the hands of the states. With the provision that the industry not engage in boycotts, intimidation, coercion, or "unduly" discriminatory practices, this law exempted the industry from most other provisions of the Sherman, Clayton, and Federal Trade Commission Acts. Thus the McCarran Act granted a reprieve to the system of state regulation, which closely controls the terms under which insurance, particularly property and liability lines, can be promoted and sold.

The most visible, and often the most vexing, power of insurance commissioners is their authority to regulate rates. While most businesses can set prices according to market conditions, antitrust laws prohibit them from colluding to raise prices. Thus the competition of independent firms operating in the same industry serves to control prices. The antitrust exemption for insurance firms, however, enables them to set prices in concert through rating bureaus. The public interest in preventing insurers from abusing this privilege provides one traditional justification of rate regulation.

The specter of destructive rate wars originally inspired rate regulation. By undercutting prices, stronger insurers could force weaker insurers out of business and increase their share of the market. While lower prices benefit consumers, the insolvency of an insurer can bring great harm. The early years of this century witnessed such insurance rate wars and prompted rate regulation to protect the public by promoting insurer stability. The bankruptcies of several airlines in the wake of deregulation illustrates the same concern, but a corporation's inability to honor an airline ticket or bonus certificate generally harms the public much less than the inability to honor an insurance claim. Thus rate regulation may be defined as a means of preventing rates that are too high, too low, or even too quickly changed.

In theory, a free market establishes an equilibrium price at which there are no unsatisfied buyers or sellers. If conditions change, the market responds automatically and establishes a new price that continues to clear the market. Insurance regulators strive to set rates at the same level that would prevail if a competitive market for insurance existed. However, no person can claim that omniscience. The time lag in the rate approval process presents another drawback. Finally, regulators are subject to political pressures, and while the marketplace may suggest one course of action, the ballot box may suggest another.

If regulators authorize rates that are either too low or too high in terms of market equilibrium, then other problems appear in the marketplace. These may lead to cumbersome administrative correctives. The consequences in the market of artificially regulated price levels are shortages and surpluses. For required insurance coverages, however, the demand is essentially fixed, and administrative solutions may be needed when the market is not in equilibrium. Thus artificially low rates generally lead to a significant residual market serviced as a condition of operating in the voluntary market.

If regulation restricts insurance rates in a particular state to a level less than one required to clear the market, insurers tighten underwriting standards in an attempt to write only profitable business. As a result, some consumers cannot obtain insurance in this voluntary market. Exhibit 5-2 illustrates this result. The intersection of the supply curve S_1 and the demand curve D represents the original equilibrium in the market. The horizontal line at P_1 shows the rate level approved by regulators exactly at the original equilibrium price. If, however, inflation or deteriorating loss experience raises costs and regulators do not approve rate increases, insurers will reduce supply from S_1 to S_2. P_2 and Q_2 represent the new equilibrium price and quantity. However, since the market equilibrium price is now above the regulated ceiling price, the market will not clear. The difference between Q_1 and Q_3 shows the number of unsatisfied buyers of insurance.

Where the availability of required insurance has become a significant problem, states have created assigned risk plans or other shared market facilities. These plans provide the insurance that cannot be obtained in the voluntary market and allocate the losses among the insurers writing business in the state. The more depressed the rate level, the more the voluntary market shrinks, throwing an increasing portion of the business into the residual market. In such situations, states often find in necessary to establish a bureaucratic system to regulate the market.

REGULATION FOR SOCIAL OBJECTIVES

Before the 1960s, much of the emphasis of regulatory activity was on specific industries. Public utilities were regulated because they tended to be natural monopolies. Transportation was regulated because

Exhibit 5-2

Effect of a Restrictive Rate Regulation

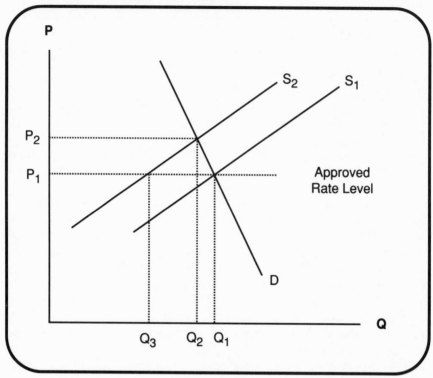

people believed that unconstrained competition would not be in the national interest. Banking and insurance were regulated because they too were considered to be of such great consequence to the national welfare that it was not prudent to allow them to be regulated simply by market forces. While there has been some significant diminution in the extent of this industry-specific regulation in the 1970s and 1980s, there has also been a tremendous increase in a different type of regulation. Concern with the environment and other aspects of the "quality of life" began to stir popular interest in resolving these issues through political action rather than in the marketplace. Special interest groups, around which particular concerns were allowed to coalesce, grew in importance.

Issue-Oriented Regulation

The regulatory agencies that arose in response to this popular movement had a different character from previous regulatory agencies.

The new agencies were constituted to address particular social concerns that cut across traditional industry lines—pollution of the environment, for example, rather than with the steel industry. The Environmental Protection Agency, the federal agency created in 1970 to address environmental concerns, did not zero in on the steel industry; instead, it focused on some particular region and proceeded to regulate all agents who contributed to the level of pollution in that region.

Similarly, the Equal Employment Opportunity Commission regulates the relationship between employer and employee, irrespective of the particular industry to which these individuals belong. The commissions and agencies became issue-oriented rather than industry-oriented. While older regulatory agencies had been specialists in the peculiar economic characteristics of their particular industry, the social interest agencies and commissions frequently did not have any particular expertise in the industries on which they had an impact. This inexperience made the measurement of costs even more problematic than it had always been for the industry-focused agencies.

While cost assessments were difficult, the evaluation of benefits was surely no easier. Much of the issue-oriented regulation addresses precisely the area of externalities. Pollution is a problem because private property rights in the environment are not well-developed. As a result, much of the polluting activity is never explicitly priced in markets. However, prices must be put on these activities if costs are to be compared to benefits.

Similar problems exist in the area of health and safety. Again, the problem is one of market failure. Usually the source of the failure is the unavailability or unreliability of information. Regulating health and safety certainly imposes some resource costs on the economy. Producers are certainly aware of the extent to which their costs have risen as a consequence of having to comply with federal, state, and local regulations. Consumers are only indirectly aware of these costs because some part of them is simply absorbed into the prices of commodities. The benefits of improved health and safety, an improved level of environmental quality, or of an end to discrimination, while certainly real, tend to be fairly dispersed and almost impossible to measure.

While most people recognize the significant potential for improvement in the quality of life by mitigating the effects of major externalities in the economic resource allocation process, it is less clear that actual regulation has, in fact, improved the quality of life. The problem has several dimensions. First, there is the problem of measurement. How can we evaluate rationally the benefits and costs of the things escaping the market, which, therefore, are not explicitly priced? Second, how can we move the unregulated market solution toward one where the marginal costs equal the marginal benefits? Regulation is only one of the possible answers to that problem, and it is not obvious that it is always the best. The true test is the resource cost of the regulation. Perhaps the information that is required could be more efficiently collected and acted on in a decentralized fashion. Third, how can we motivate the regulators themselves? Last, but not least, how can we solve the problem that costs and benefits, even if they could be measured, still depend on the income distribution?

Concern with the degradation of the quality of the environment has grown rapidly over the past several decades. This concern probably results from several related phenomena. Real incomes in the United States have risen, and the appreciation of environmental quality seems to increase with income. Because our leisure time has increased, we are much more likely to have the time to notice our environment. In addition, our society has become much more industrial, and most industrial processes produce waste as a by-product. The fact that most of these by-products manage to escape the market mechanism (in other words, that production creates externalities) is in large part responsible for the pollution problem. Externalities distort the signals that markets send. When all resource costs are not borne by the producer, output increases to an inefficient level. A discrepancy between social valuation and private valuation of resources results. Since price fails to reflect the marginal social valuation of all the resources that are required for production, relative scarcity is no longer reflected by prices. Consumers are then tempted to overconsume.

Exhibit 5-3 shows the market demand for some commodity. The demand is presumed to reflect the marginal social valuation of additional units of this commodity. It also shows two marginal cost curves. MCP measures the private marginal costs incurred by the producers of the commodity; MCS measures the social marginal cost. The vertical difference between these two marginal cost curves measures costs incurred in the production of the commodity, but that the producer can escape. They are the costs to society at large of the air pollution, water pollution, or reduced recreational open space the production process produces as an unpriced by-product.

If the market is competitive, the unregulated equilibrium will be at a price of P_1 and an output level of Q_1. However, at this output level, while firms have maximized profit, society as a whole is not as well off as possible. The marginal social cost has exceeded the marginal social benefit since output was expanded past Q_2. Every unit of output past Q_2 added more social cost than the social benefit it produced. Social welfare has been declining. The invisible hand has failed. Private profit maximization has not led to social welfare maximization.

In principle, there are a number of ways in which this distortion

Exhibit 5-3
Market Equilibrium with and without Externalities

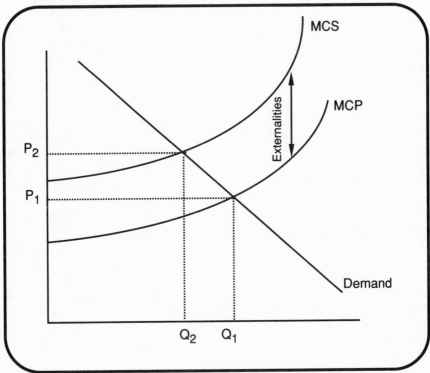

could be corrected. We could continue to rely on decentralized decisionmaking in competitive markets. This, however, requires that we somehow force all inputs, including environmental resources such as clean air or water, to be auctioned. If we could somehow reconstitute the laws of property so that property rights in environmental resources could be created, producers who wished to use these resources in their production processes would have to compensate the owners of those rights for any damage done to their property. In this case, there would be no difference between marginal private and marginal social costs. The costs of the environmental damage would be borne fully by the producer, and profit maximizing output level would be Q_2.

While there undoubtedly are instances when this approach would work, practical applications are probably limited. The owner of a pond or small lake can negotiate with producers for the right to pollute. But even here, there are probably secondary externalities that will continue to escape the pricing mechanism. Migrating wildlife will probably be affected by a seriously polluted pond and may well spread whatever ill effects are associated with the pollution beyond the immediate area. More generally, however, property rights probably would not work well because of the essentially public goods nature of many of our resources, especially the atmosphere.

Cynics have asserted that the concern with the quality of the environment, especially the nonurbanized areas of this country, prevails largely among the wealthy city dwellers anxious to preserve the rustic quality of their vacation retreats. Local residents of these rural areas are frequently far more interested in the availability of well-paying jobs. Yet, environmentalists frequently succeed in restricting the economic development of these areas. One's evaluation of the importance of a clean environment is a function of one's income. Pollution in Appalachia is far less a concern for the unemployed than it is for the visitors and the local residents who happen to be employed.

The effectiveness record of the new regulation for improving the quality of life is uneven. It ranges from substantial reductions in certain types of pollution and the reduction in highway fatalities at least partly attributable to the work of the National Highway Traffic Safety Administration all the way to the doubtful effect of OSHA's regulation of ladder specifications. Regardless of their effectiveness, however, these improvements have been achieved at some cost. Only a small portion of the cost is measured by actual federal outlays for the administrative and enforcement machinery of the regulatory agencies and commissions. These regulations have also imposed significant costs on the affected firms.

Protectionist Regulation

Not all regulation is designed to deal with externalities or monopoly power. Some has been applied to industries that might well have had many of the characteristics of competitive industries. Frequently such regulation is purportedly designed for social purposes. Often, however, the effect, if not the intent, is to protect or to augment the wealth of the regulated at the expense of the population at large. Examples include the regulation of farm prices and output and the regulation of the trucking industry as well as various forms of occupational licensing.

The farm regions have historically had an influence on national politics, particularly in the Senate, that is far greater than their number or economic power would suggest. To protect the incomes of farmers, Congress has seen fit to enact a system of rules and laws (farm programs) that protect many of this nation's farmers from unbridled competition. Import duties and quotas reduce the extent to which foreign suppliers can drive down domestic price. Foreign aid programs increase the demand for U.S.-produced foodstuffs. Favorable tax treatment of farm incomes and assets (farm lands) reduced the costs of farming. Activities by the U.S. Department of Agriculture to improve farming techniques also reduce the costs of production.

Of course, the favorable effects of foreign trade restrictions and inducement (for example, below market-rate loans for those foreigners who wish to finance purchases of U.S. produced goods) are not restricted to farmers. The automobile industry at one time was insulated from foreign competitors through import quotas on automobiles. Domestic content legislation has protected workers in some industries from competition by foreign workers.

Until recently, entry and prices in the trucking industry were closely regulated. Although there is little evidence that the trucking industry is not inherently competitive, it has been heavily regulated since it became a major force in surface freight transportation. The original motivation for this regulation was to protect the competitive position of the nation's railroads. Over the years regulation was maintained in order to support the asset value of operating rights. Although the purported reason behind the regulation was the protection of small shippers and small communities, there is significant evidence that the value of regulation to these groups was far exceeded by the costs imposed on the rest of the user groups.

By reducing competition in most markets, the ICC forced truckers to engage in a series of inefficient and wasteful practices. For example, carriers were frequently certified to carry only specific commodities between specific cities. More often than not, such arrangements forced the carriers to return to their city of origin without cargo. Such lopsided hauling practices imposed rather significant resource costs on society and certainly increased the cost of trucking above what it would otherwise have been.

While occupational licensing is almost always defended as a necessary method for the protection of consumers from incompetent practitioners, such licensing also restricts entry into the profession and thereby allows the incumbent practitioners to raise their prices. There are many examples of this practice. Licenses are required for insurance agents, lawyers, funeral directors, barbers, neurosurgeons, and high school teachers. While it is certainly desirable to keep incompetents out of these and other professions, the vehemence with which some licensed groups oppose periodic competency tests suggests that entry restriction as well as quality control can be a significant motivation.

Regulating price and output in markets that could otherwise be at least nearly competitive seems certain to entail efficiency costs, while the benefits of such regulation to the public are less clear. When prices in such industries are regulated above those that would yield market participants a normal rate of return on their investment, other types of competition tend to proliferate. If airlines are not allowed to engage in price competition, for example, they compete on the basis of service quality. Flight frequency increases, and inflight meals become fancier. While such service and amenities may well be desired by some customers, others who would rather substitute lower fares will be prevented from doing so by the regulation. Even the airlines themselves may not reap very large monopoly profits in such situations. For as long as there are some competing carriers in a market and as long as only price is regulated, the airlines tend to compete on the basis of service, thereby increasing their costs until marginal costs equal marginal revenue (rather than increasing their output or reducing their price until marginal revenue equals marginal cost).

Another source of inefficiency is that regulatory agencies frequently set prices in such a way as to protect even some of the less efficient firms in a regulated industry. The setting of prices based on the average costs (rather than the best practice costs) reduces the pressure on industry members to seek the most efficient ways of doing business.

SUMMARY

Although rational choices in a perfectly competitive market lead to efficient results, regulation often constrains the choices. One reason for regulation is that certain imperfect markets left to themselves do not lead to the most efficient or desirable results. In such cases of market failure, regulation serves as a corrective. The financial sector of the economy is also highly regulated in the interest of financial stability. In addition to market failure and financial stability, however, social objectives often lead to many other forms of regulation even though there may be no economic need for them.

There are essentially two approaches to regulatory correctives for market failures. One approach strives to inhibit the development of market power. Antitrust laws enable the government to prevent mergers or business combinations that would produce excessive concentration in an industry. Antitrust laws also prohibit anticompetitive behavior, such as predatory pricing, price fixing, price discrimination, and tying contracts. In cases of monopoly, however, no competition exists. Because monopolists can restrict output and raise prices, monopoly regulation concentrates on setting reasonable rates of return that allow the monopoly to stay in business without exploiting consumers. This goal presents a considerable administrative challenge to regulatory agencies.

Financial institutions are subject to a special form of regulation designed to assure their solvency, to control the financial system, and to protect consumers from misinformation. Banks must meet the requirements of the Federal Reserve System and limit their activities to those permitted under the law. Bank examinations help to detect a deteriorating financial condition, and deposit insurance mechanisms protect depositors when bank failures do occur. State regulation of insurance companies incorporates many similar features, including financial examinations, limitations on investment policy, and consumer protection. Since the McCarran-Ferguson Act exempts insurance companies from many provisions of the federal antitrust laws, state regulators also focus on setting allowable insurance rates.

While attempts to correct market failures and to preserve financial stability lead to regulation of specific industries, social objectives usually lead to regulation that applies to all businesses generally. The agencies and commissions responsible for this type of regulation tend to be issue-oriented rather than industry-oriented. They face even greater challenges than agencies responsible for regulating specific industries because of the volume of information required and the difficulty of measuring the costs and benefits of particular regulations. For example, pollution occurs largely because of externalities. Although the market allocates resources, it does not capture the costs of cleaning the environment and pass them on to the polluters. Regulation can attempt to prohibit defined types of pollution or to impose the costs on the polluters, but enforcement of such regulations requires adequate administrative procedures and staff. At some point the regulators must ask whether the benefits exceed the costs. It is difficult, however, to put a price tag on the long-term benefit of a clean environment, and different people hold different opinions on the subject. In fact, some types of regulation may purport to be in the public interest, but primarily benefit a special interest group. Free markets do not exist in agriculture, for example, because it is government policy to protect the income of farmers from the extremes of the swings in the market. Certain occupations require licensing, which protects the public from unqualified practitioners, but it also protects the interest of the licensed. Even though such policies have economic consequences, whether they are appropriate must be decided on other grounds. Like all economic decisionmaking, regulation involves making rational choices from among competing alternatives, but it too is subject to constraints.

Chapter Notes

1. Murray L. Weidenbaum, "Government Power and Business Performance," in *The United States in the 1980s*, ed. Peter Dunignan and Alvin Robushka (Palo Alto, CA: Hoover Institution, 1980), p. 200.
2. Paul L. Joskow, "Cartels, Competition and Regulation in the Property-Liability Insurance Industry." *The Bell Journal of Economics and Management Science*, Vol. 4, Autumn 1973, pp. 391-394.

Bibliography

Becker, Gary S. *The Economic Approach to Human Behavior.* Chicago: University of Chicago Press, 1976.

Buchanan, James M. "The Economic Theory of Politics Reborn." *Challenge,* March/April 1988, p. 4.

Buchanan, James M. and Tullock, Gordon. *The Calculus of Consent.* Ann Arbor, MI: University of Michigan Press, 1962.

Hirshleifer, Jack. "Economics from a Biological Viewpoint." *The Journal of Law and Economics,* April 1977, pp. 1-52.

_____. "The Expanding Domain of Economics," *The American Economic Review,* December 1985, p. 53.

Joskow, Paul L. "Cartels, Competition and Regulation in the Property-Liability Insurance Industry." *The Bell Journal of Economics and Management Science,* Vol. 4, Autumn 1973, pp. 391- 394.

Simon, Herbert A. "Theories of Decision-Making in Economics and Behavioral Science." *The American Economic Review,* June 1959, p. 263.

Smith, Adam. *The Wealth of Nations.* New York: The Modern Library, 1937.

Weidenbaum, Murray L. "Government Power and Business Performance," *The United States in the 1980s,* ed. Peter Dunignan and Alvin Robushka. Palo Alto, CA: Hoover Institution, 1980.

Index